The Daffodil
Poetry Book

Dedicated to
KATHARINE TYNAN

LEARNIN'

Labour for learnin' afore ye grow old,
For learnin' is better nor silver and gold!
Silver and gold it will vanish away,
But learnin' itself it will never decay,
And a man without learnin' wearin' good clothes
Is like a gold ring in a pig's nose.

PATRICK MACGILL.

The Daffodil Poetry Book

Compiled by Ethel L. Fowler

Granger Index Reprint Series

BOOKS FOR LIBRARIES PRESS
FREEPORT, NEW YORK

First Published 1920
Reprinted 1970 by arrangement with
Sidgwick & Jackson, Ltd.

STANDARD BOOK NUMBER:
8369-6180-3

LIBRARY OF CONGRESS CATALOG CARD NUMBER:
70-128153

PREFACE

IT is with great pleasure as well as with confidence that I recommend this new collection of poems to the notice of all lovers of poetry, but especially to those who desire to arouse interest in the young, and to introduce them to the charm and spirit of humanity found in the writings of so many of our modern poets.

I do this with great pleasure because Miss Fowler is both a member of my staff and a teacher who understands the minds of young people, as this little book of poetry proves, for the majority of the poems selected have been learnt and appreciated by many of the pupils in this school.

I commend it with confidence, although so many poetry books for the young are already in use, because it seems to me these poems, both in subject-matter and in choice, are especially marked by a living freshness, by great originality, and by a sympathetic understanding of the human heart.

There are two further characteristics I should like also to mention : its introduction of a great number of fascinating little poems by comparatively new and therefore less known authors, and its methodical arrangement, which enables any particular kind of poem to be easily found, as the selections are most carefully grouped and graded. Each part opens with some delightful and finished verses setting forth the fresh spirit of nature, which then are followed by charming poems of fancy and imagination, and closes with ballads, legendary tales, and stories of romance.

E. BEATRICE HARRISON,
M.A., T.C.D., and Girton College, Cambridge;
Head Mistress of the Municipal Secondary School for Girls, Ipswich

May 1920.

COMPILER'S NOTE

THE Compiler wishes to express her sincere thanks to Katharine Tynan (Mrs. Hinkson) for her encouragement and help during the preparation of this book; to Miss E. B. Harrison, without whose far-sighted sympathy such a work would have been impossible; and to Miss E. M. Cornell for much valuable advice and assistance.

INDEX OF AUTHORS

⁎ *Authors, their representatives, and Publishers, to whom the Compiler desires to make grateful acknowledgements for permission to use copyright poems, are named in parentheses after the Author's name.*

	PAGE
ALLINGHAM, WILLIAM (Mrs. Allingham and Messrs. Longmans, Green & Co.)	
30. Kate o' Belashanny	35
34. The Maids of Elfin-Mere.	43
ANONYMOUS (No. 15, the Proprietors of *Punch*; No. 49, Messrs. J. M. Dent & Sons, Ltd.)	
15. Saint George of England	16
42. The Twa Sisters o' Binnorie (*Old Ballad*)	55
43. Fair Helen of Kirconnel (*Old Ballad*)	59
44. Lord Randal (*Old Ballad*)	60
49. St. George and the Dragon (from *Everyman and Other Interludes*)	76
ARNOLD, MATTHEW	
35. The Neckan	44
73. Requiescat	102
BEECHING, HENRY CHARLES (Mrs. Beeching and Mr. John Lane)	
20. Going Down Hill on a Bicycle	23
BLAKE, WILLIAM	
52. To Spring	82
61. To Morning	92
76. And did those Feet (from *Milton*)	104
88. The Tiger	119

INDEX OF AUTHORS

	PAGE
BRIDGES, ROBERT (Mr. John Murray)	
4. The Palm Willow	3
55. The Pinks	84
56. North Wind in October	85
67. In Still Midsummer Night	97
BROOKE, RUPERT (Author's Literary Executor and Sidgwick & Jackson, Ltd.)	
51. Song ("All suddenly the wind comes soft")	81
75. The Soldier	104
78. The Dead ("Blow out, you bugles")	107
BROWN, THOMAS EDWARD (Messrs. Macmillan & Co., Ltd.)	
96. My Garden	127
BROWNING, ROBERT (Mr. John Murray)	
47. The Boy and the Angel	67
62. Day (from *Pippa Passes*)	92
101. The Guardian Angel (extract)	134
CANTON, WILLIAM (Author and Messrs. J. M. Dent & Sons, Ltd.)	
12. Carol (from *The Invisible Playmate*)	13
CHESSON, NORA (W. H. Chesson, Esq.)	
27. The Short Cut to Rosses	30
CLARK, DUDLEY (Author and the Editor of the *Times*)	
16. Called Up	18
COWPER, WILLIAM	
89. The Silkworm	120
CRIPPS, ARTHUR SHEARLY (Author and Mr. B. H. Blackwell)	
17. A Refrain	20
DE LA MARE, WALTER (Author, per Mr. J. B. Pinker)	
9. Berries	9
22. Tartary	25
25. The Mocking Fairy	28
68. The Truants	98
DOBSON, AUSTIN (Author and Messrs. Kegan Paul & Co., Ltd.)	
94. The Milkmaid	124

INDEX OF AUTHORS

	PAGE
DRINKWATER, JOHN (Author and Sidgwick & Jackson, Ltd.)	
2. The Miracle	2
50. January Dusk	81
54. Buds	83
84. Morning Thanksgiving	112
106. In Lady Street	152
F., W. M. E. (by courtesy of the Editor of *Colour*)	
3. A February Song	3
FOWLER, ETHEL LOUISA	
100. The Roadside Pines	133
GALES, RICHARD LAWSON (Author and Messrs. Simpkin, Marshall & Co., Ltd.)	
13. Waiting for the Kings	14
48. A Ballad of St. Christopher	71
GARSTIN, CROSBIE (Author and Sidgwick & Jackson, Ltd.)	
53. Rondeau	83
GORE-BOOTH, EVA (Author and Messrs. Longmans, Green & Co.)	
71. The Little Waves of Breffny	100
GRENFELL, JULIAN (Lady Desborough and the Editor of the *Times*)	
77. Into Battle	105
HARDY, THOMAS (Author and Messrs. Macmillan & Co., Ltd.)	
74. The Going of the Battery	102
81. Song of the Soldiers' Wives	109
104. The Souls of the Slain	145
HARVEY, FREDERICK WILLIAM (Author and Sidgwick & Jackson, Ltd.)	
87. Ducks	116
HERBERT, GEORGE	
86. Virtue	115
HERRICK, ROBERT	
60. An Ode of the Birth of our Saviour	91
85. A Thanksgiving to God for His House	113
HUNT, JAMES HENRY LEIGH	
7. Garden Lilies	6

INDEX OF AUTHORS

	PAGE

INGELOW, JEAN (Messrs. Longmans, Green & Co.)
    46. Persephone 64

JENKINS, ELINOR (Lady Jenkins and Sidgwick & Jackson, Ltd.)
    79. A Legend of Ypres 107

JOHNSON, LIONEL (Mr. Elkin Mathews)
    105. By the Statue of King Charles at Charing Cross . 150

KEATS, JOHN
    39. La Belle Dame sans Merci 50
    70. Faery Song 99
    91. To a Cat 122
    108. To the Poets 158

LANGBRIDGE, ROSAMOND (Author and the Editor of the *Westminster Gazette*)
    66. Phosphorescence 95

LEE-HAMILTON, EUGENE (The Walter Scott Publishing Co., Ltd.)
    26. The Death of Puck [1] 29

LETTS, WINIFRED M. (Author and Mr. John Murray)
    5. Spring, the Travelling Man 4

MACGILL, PATRICK [2] (Author and Messrs. Heath Cranton, Ltd.)
    29. The Farmer's Boy 33
    99. The Pines (from *A Little Book of Irish Verse*) . . 132

MARSTON, PHILIP BOURKE (per Coulson Kernahan, Esq.)
    8. The Rose and the Wind 7

MARVELL, ANDREW
    90. The Nymph complaining for the Death of her Fawn (extract) 121
    97. The Garden 128

---

[1] From *Poems by Eugene Lee-Hamilton* (The Canterbury Poets, 1s. 6d.).

[2] 'Learnin',' facing the title-page, is taken from Mr. MacGill's *Glenmornan*, by permission of Author, and Publishers, Messrs. Herbert Jenkins. Ltd.

INDEX OF AUTHORS

	PAGE

MONRO, HAROLD (Author and the Poetry Book Shop)
   24. Overheard on a Saltmarsh 27

MORRIS, WILLIAM (Miss May Morris and Messrs. Longmans, Green & Co.)
   38. Two Red Roses across the Moon 48
   58. Carol (from *The Land East of the Sun and West of the Moon*) 86

NOYES, ALFRED (per Messrs. A. P. Watt & Son and Messrs. Blackwood & Sons)
   6. The Barrel Organ (extract) 5
   11. Snow (from *A Friend of Carlyle*) 13
   102. Sherwood 136

O'NEILL, MOIRA (Author and Messrs. Blackwood & Sons)
   31. Birds (from *Songs of the Glens of Antrim*) . . 37
   72. A Broken Song (from *Songs of the Glens of Antrim*) . 101
   95. Johneen (from *Songs of the Glens of Antrim*) . . 126

PEACOCK, THOMAS LOVE
   18. Bold Robin 20
   19. The War-Song of Dinas Vawr 22

POE, EDGAR ALLAN
   36. Eldorado 47
   40. The Haunted Palace 52
   41. Annabel Lee 53
   45. Lenore 62

ROSSETTI, CHRISTINA GEORGINA
   32. Birds of Paradise 38

SIDGWICK, FRANK (Author and Sidgwick & Jackson, Ltd.)
   59. A Christmas Legend 88

SHAKESPEARE, WILLIAM
   92. Sonnet CXXX ("My mistress' eyes are nothing like the sun") 123
   93. Sonnet XCIX ("The forward violet thus did I chide") 124

SHELLEY, PERCY BYSSHE
   10. Autumn: a Dirge 12
   63. To Night 93
   98. The Question 130

	PAGE
STEPHENS, JAMES (Author and Messrs. Maunsel & Co., Ltd.)	
64. Donnybrook	94
STEVENSON, ROBERT LOUIS (Messrs. Longmans, Green & Co.)	
21. From a Railway Carriage	24
TENNYSON, ALFRED (LORD) (Messrs. Macmillan & Co., Ltd., for No. 14)	
14. Song (from *The Coming of Arthur*)	15
103. The Lady of Shalott	138
107. Tithonus	155
THOMPSON, FRANCIS (Mrs. Meynell and Messrs. Burns, Oates & Washbourne, Ltd.)	
33. Cheated Elsie	40
57. To a Snowflake	86
TURNER, WALTER JAMES (Author and Sidgwick & Jackson, Ltd.)	
23. Romance	26
TYNAN, KATHARINE (Mrs. Hinkson) (Author)	
1. Daffodil	1
80. A Girl's Song	108
VAUGHAN, HENRY	
82. Peace	110
WATSON, SIR WILLIAM (Mr. John Lane)	
37. The Lute-Player	48
WORDSWORTH, WILLIAM	
65. Sleep	95
YEATS, WILLIAM BUTLER (per Messrs. A. P. Watt & Son, and Messrs. Macmillan & Co., Ltd).	
28. The Stolen Child	31
69. The Voice (from *The Land of Heart's Desire*)	99
83. The Lake Isle of Innisfree	111

THE
DAFFODIL POETRY BOOK
PART I

1. DAFFODIL

Who passes down the wintry street?
      Hey, ho, daffodil!
A sudden flame of gold and sweet.

With sword of emerald girt so meet,
And golden gay from head to feet.

How are you here this wintry day?
      Hey, ho, daffodil!
Your radiant fellows yet delay.

No windflower dances scarlet gay,
Nor crocus-flame lights up the way.

What land of cloth o' gold and green,
      Hey, ho, daffodil!
Cloth o' gold with the green between,

Was that you left but yestere'en
To light a gloomy world and mean?

King trumpeter to Flora queen,
      Hey, ho, daffodil!
Blow, and the golden jousts begin.

                    Katharine Tynan.

2. THE MIRACLE

Come, sweetheart, listen, for I have a thing
    Most wonderful to tell you—news of spring.

Albeit winter still is in the air,
And the earth troubled, and the branches bare,

Yet down the fields to-day I saw her pass—
The spring—her feet went shining through the grass.

She touched the ragged hedgerows—I have seen
Her finger-prints, most delicately green;

And she has whispered to the crocus leaves,
And to the garrulous sparrows in the eaves.

Swiftly she passed and shyly, and her fair
Young face was hidden in her cloudy hair.

She would not stay, her season is not yet,
But she has re-awakened, and has set

The sap of all the world astir, and rent
Once more the shadows of our discontent.

Triumphant news—a miracle I sing—
The everlasting miracle of spring.

                        John Drinkwater.

3. A FEBRUARY SONG

THE storm-cock in the apple-trees at frosty dawn
  is heard—
Man planted apple-trees, but God gave the bird ;
God gave the winter and the long, dark hours,
And man must plod along the road and learn to trust
  His powers.

In the garden, crocuses, yellow points like flame,
"Hymen's Torch" their beautiful and half-forgotten
  name ;
Man set the crocuses, but God made them blow,
Living tapers from His hands to blossom and to glow.

Candles for Candlemas of every length and size
Twinkling in the duskiness like planets from the
  skies ;
Man made the candles, but God taught the way,
And He will lead the Winter night through Spring to
  Summer day.

W. M. E. F.

4. THE PALM WILLOW

SEE, whirling snow sprinkles the starvèd fields,
  The birds have stayed to sing ;
No covert yet their fairy harbour yields.
    When cometh Spring ?
Ah ! in their tiny throats what songs unborn
    Are quenched each morn.

The lenten lilies, through the frost that push,
    Their yellow heads withhold:
The woodland willow stands a lonely bush
    Of nebulous gold;
There the Spring-goddess cowers in faint attire
    Of frightened fire.   *Robert Bridges.*

5. SPRING, THE TRAVELLING MAN

Spring, the Travelling Man, has been here,
    Here in the glen;
He must have passed by in the grey of the dawn,
When only the robin and wren
Were awake,
Watching out with their bright little eyes
In the midst of the brake.
The rabbits, maybe, heard him pass,
Stepping light on the grass,
Whistling careless and gay at the break o' the day.
Then the blackthorn to give him delight
Put on raiment of white:
And, all for his sake,
The gorse on the hill, where he rested an hour,
Grew bright with a splendour of flower.
My grief, that I was not aware
Of himself being there;
It is I would have given my dower
To have seen him set forth,
Whistling careless and gay in the grey of the morn,
By gorse bush and fraughan and thorn,
On his way to the north.   *Winifred Letts.*

6. THE BARREL ORGAN (Extract)

Go down to Kew in lilac-time, in lilac-time, in lilac-time;
Go down to Kew in lilac-time (it isn't far from London!)
And you shall wander hand in hand with love in summer's wonderland;
Go down to Kew in lilac-time (it isn't far from London!)

The cherry trees are seas of bloom and soft perfume and sweet perfume,
The cherry trees are seas of bloom (and oh! so near to London!)
And there they say, when dawn is high, and all the world's a blaze of sky,
The cuckoo, though he's very shy, will sing a song for London.

The nightingale is rather rare and yet they say you'll hear him there
At Kew, at Kew, in lilac-time (and oh! so near to London!)
The linnet and the throstle, too, and after dark the long halloo
And golden-eyed *tu-whit*, *tu-whoo* of owls that ogle London.

For Noah hardly knew a bird of any kind that isn't heard
At Kew, at Kew, in lilac-time (and oh! so near to London!)

And when the rose begins to pout, and all the chestnut spires are out,
You'll hear the rest without a doubt, all chorusing for London :—

Come down to Kew in lilac-time, in lilac-time, in lilac-time,
Come down to Kew in lilac-time (it isn't far from London !)
And you shall wander hand in hand with love in summer's wonderland ;
Come down to Kew in lilac-time (it isn't far from London !)

Alfred Noyes.

7. GARDEN LILIES

We are lilies fair,
    The flower of virgin light ;
Nature held us forth, and said,
    " Lo, my thoughts of white ! "

Ever since then, angels
    Hold us in their hands ;
You may see them where they take,
    In pictures, their sweet stands.

Like the garden's angels
    Likewise do we seem ;
And not the less for being crowned
    With a golden dream.

Could you see around us
    The sweet fragrant air,
You would see it pale with bliss
    To hold a thing so fair.

Leigh Hunt.

8. THE ROSE AND THE WIND
DAWN

The Rose:

WHEN think you comes the Wind,
    The Wind that kisses me and is so kind?
Lo! how the Lily sleeps! her sleep is light;
Would I were like the Lily, pale and white!
Will the Wind come?

The Beech:
Perchance for you too soon.

The Rose:
If not, how could I live until the noon?
What, think you, Beech-tree, makes the Wind delay?
Why comes he not at breaking of the day?

The Beech:
Hush, child, and like the Lily, go to sleep.

The Rose:
You know I cannot.

The Beech:
Nay then, do not weep.   *(After a pause)*
Your lover comes, be happy now, O Rose!
He softly through my bending branches goes.
Soon he shall come and you shall feel his kiss.

The Rose:
Already my flushed heart grows faint with bliss,
Love, I have longed for you through all the night.

The Wind:
And I to kiss your petals warm and bright.

The Rose:
Laugh round me, Love, and kiss me; all is well.
Nay, have no fear, the Lily will not tell.

MORNING

The Rose:
'Twas dawn when first you came ; and now the sun
Shines brightly, and the dews of dawn are done.
'Tis well you take me so in your embrace ;
But lay me back again into my place,
For I am worn, perhaps with bliss extreme.

The Wind:
Nay, you must wake, Love, from this foolish dream.

The Rose:
'Tis you, Love, who seem changed ; your laugh is loud ;
And 'neath your stormy kiss my head is bowed.
O Love, O Wind, a space will you not spare?

The Wind:
Not while your petals are so soft and fair.

The Rose:
My buds are blind with leaves, they cannot see.—
O Love, O Wind, will you not pity me?

EVENING

The Beech:
O Wind, a word with you before you pass;
What did you to the Rose that on the grass
Broken she lies and pale, who loved you so?

The Wind:
Roses must live and love, and winds must blow.

Philip Bourke Marston.

9. BERRIES

There was an old woman
   Went blackberry picking
Along the hedges
  From Weep to Wicking.
Half a pottle—
  No more she had got,
When out steps a Fairy
  From her green grot;
And says, "Well, Jill,
  Would 'ee pick 'ee mo?"
And Jill, she curtseys,
  And looks just so.
"Be off," says the Fairy,
  "As quick as you can,
Over the meadows
  To the little green lane,
That dips to the hayfields
  Of Farmer Grimes:
I've berried those hedges
  A score of times;

Bushel on bushel
   I'll promise 'ee, Jill,
This side of supper
   If 'ee pick with a will."
She glints very bright,
   And speaks her fair;
Then lo, and behold!
   She had faded in air.

Be sure Old Goodie
   She trots betimes
Over the meadows
   To Farmer Grimes.
And never was queen
   With jewellery rich
As those same hedges
   From twig to ditch;
Like Dutchmen's coffers,
   Fruit, thorn, and flower—
They shone like William
   And Mary's bower.
And be sure Old Goodie
   Went back to Weep,
So tired with her basket
   She scarce could creep.

When she comes in the dusk
   To her cottage door,
There's Towser wagging
   As never before,

To see his Missus
   So glad to be
Come from her fruit-picking
   Back to he.
As soon as next morning
   Dawn was grey,
The pot on the hob
   Was simmering away;
And all in a stew
   And a hugger-mugger
Towser and Jill
   A-boiling of sugar,
And the dark clear fruit
   That from Faërie came,
For syrup and jelly
   And blackberry jam.

Twelve jolly gallipots
   Jill put by;
And one little teeny one,
   One inch high;
And that she's hidden
   A good thumb deep,
Half way over
   From Wicking to Weep.

Walter de la Mare.

10. AUTUMN

A Dirge

THE warm sun is failing, the bleak wind is wailing,
    The bare boughs are sighing, the pale flowers
  are dying,
        And the year
On the earth her deathbed, in a shroud of leaves dead,
        Is lying.
    Come, months, come away,
    From November to May,
    In your saddest array;
    Follow the bier
    Of the dead cold year,
And like dim shadows watch by her sepulchre.

The chill rain is falling, the nipt worm is crawling,
The rivers are swelling, the thunder is knelling
        For the year;
The blithe swallows are flown, and the lizards each
  gone
        To his dwelling.
    Come, months, come away;
    Put on white, black, and grey;
    Let your light sisters play—
    Ye, follow the bier
    Of the dead cold year,
And make her grave green with tear on tear.

Percy Bysshe Shelley.

11. SNOW (*Extract*)

A PURE white mantle blotted out
    The world I used to know :
There was no scarlet in the sky
    Or on the hills below,
Gently as mercy out of heaven
    Came down the healing snow.

The trees that were so dark and bare
    Stood up in radiant white,
And the road forgot its furrowed care
    As day forgets the night,
And the new heavens and the new earth
    Lay robed in dazzling light.

And every flake that fell from heaven
    Was like an angel's kiss,
Or a feather fluttering from the wings
    Of some dear soul in bliss
Who gently leaned from that bright world
    To soothe the pain of this.

Alfred Noyes.

12. CAROL

WHEN the herds were watching
    In the midnight chill,
Came a spotless lambkin
    From the heavenly hill.

Snow was on the mountains,
   And the wind was cold,
When from God's own garden
   Dropped a rose of gold.

When 'twas bitter winter,
   Houseless and forlorn
In a star-lit stable
   Christ the Babe was born.

Welcome, heavenly lambkin;
   Welcome, golden rose;
Alleluia, Baby
   In the swaddling clothes!

William Canton.

13. WAITING FOR THE KINGS

Over the frozen plains snow-white
   The three Kings will come to-night;
We shall know by the kettle-drums
Which way the procession comes.

They have come from very far,
Following fast behind a star,
In their shimmering robes of silk,
Riding horses white as milk.

They bring through the starlit dark
Gold once hid in Noë's Ark;
They bear over snow and ice
Bags of musk and myrrh and spice.

They have heard of a wondrous thing,
That here is born a little King;
They bring treasures of great worth
To the Treasure of the earth.

When we see the Kings ride past,
Thro' the silence white and vast,
In the night will bloom, methinks,
Velvet roses and striped pinks.

When we see them all aglow,
Riding over leagues of snow,
In their robes of red and gold,
We shall never feel the cold.

We will print upon the gifts
They have borne thro' the snow-drifts,
Thro' the bitter weather wild,
Kisses for the Little Child.

Richard Lawson Gales.

14. SONG (FROM "THE COMING OF ARTHUR")

Blow trumpet, for the world is white with May;
  Blow trumpet, the long night hath roll'd away!
Blow thro' the living world—"Let the King reign."

  Shall Rome or Heathen rule in Arthur's realm?
Flash brand and lance, fall battleaxe upon helm,
Fall battleaxe, and flash brand! Let the King reign.

Strike for the King and live! his knights have heard
That God hath told the King a secret word.
Fall battleaxe, and flash brand! Let the King reign.

Blow trumpet! he will lift us from the dust.
Blow trumpet! live the strength and die the lust!
Clang battleaxe, and clash brand! Let the King reign.

Strike for the King and die! and if thou diest,
The King is King, and ever wills the highest.
Clang battleaxe, and clash brand! Let the King reign.

Blow, for our Sun is mighty in his May!
Blow, for our Sun is mightier day by day!
Clang battleaxe, and clash brand! Let the King reign.

The King will follow Christ, and we the King
In whom high God hath breathed a secret thing.
Fall battleaxe, and flash brand! Let the King reign.

Alfred Tennyson.

15. SAINT GEORGE OF ENGLAND
His Day, April 23rd

Saint George he was a fighting man, as all the tales do tell;
He fought a battle long ago, and fought it wondrous well;
With his helmet and his hauberk and his good cross-hilted sword,
Oh, he rode a-slaying Dragons to the glory of the Lord.

And when his time on earth was done he found he
    could not rest
Where the year is always Summer in the Islands of
    the Blest,
So back he came to earth again to see what he could
    do,
And they cradled him in England—
In England, April England—
Oh, they cradled him in England where the golden
    willows blew.

Saint George he was a fighting man and loved a fight-
    ing breed,
And wherever England wants him now he's ready to
    her need;
From Crecy Field to Neuve Chapelle, he's there with
    hand and sword,
And he sailed with Drake from Devon to the glory of
    the Lord.
His arm is strong to fight the wrong and break the
    tyrant's pride;
He was there when Nelson triumphed, he was there
    when Gordon died;
He sees his Red Cross ensign float on all the winds
    that blow,
And oh! his heart's in England—
In England, April England—
His heart it dreams of England, where the golden
    willows blow.

Saint George he was a fighting man, he's here and
 fighting still,
While any wrong is yet to right or Dragon yet to kill;
And faith! he's finding work this day to suit his
 war-worn sword,
For he's strafing Huns in Flanders to the glory of the
 Lord!
Saint George he is a fighting man, but, when the
 fighting's past,
And dead amidst the trampled fields the fiercest and
 the last
Of all the Dragons earth has known beneath his feet
 lies low,
Ah! his heart will turn to England—
To England, April England—
He'll come back to rest in England where the golden
 willows blow. *From " Punch."*

16. CALLED UP

Come, tumble up, Lord Nelson, the British Fleet's
 a-looming!
Come, show a leg, Lord Nelson, the guns they are
 a-booming!
'Tis a longish line of battle,—such as we did never see;
An' 'tis not the same old round-shot as was fired by
 you an' me!

What see'st thou, Sir Francis?—Strange things I see
 appearing!
What hearest thou, Sir Francis?—Strange sounds I do
 be hearing!

They are fighting in the heavens; they're at war
    beneath the sea !
Ay, their ways are mighty different from the ways
    o' you an' me !

See'st thou nought else, Sir Francis ?—I see great
    lights a-seeking !
Hearest thou nought else, Sir Francis ?—I hear thin
    wires a-speaking !
Three leagues that shot hath carried !—God, that such
    could ever be !
There's no mortal doubt, Lord Nelson—they ha'
    done wi' you and me !

Look thou again, Sir Francis !—I see the flags a-
    flapping !
Hearken once more, Sir Francis !—I hear the sticks
    a-tapping !
'Tis a sight that calls me thither !—'Tis a sound that
    bids me " Come ! "
'Tis the old Trafalgar signal !—'Tis the beating of my
    drum !

*Art thou ready, good Sir Francis ? See, they wait upon
    the Quay !*—
Praise be to God, Lord Nelson, they ha' thought of
    you an' me !

                                         Dudley Clark.

17. A REFRAIN

TELL the tune his feet beat
   On the ground all day—
Black-burnt ground and green grass
Seamed with rocks of grey—
"England," "England," "England,"
That one word they say.

Now they tread the beech-mast,
Now the ploughland's clay,
Now the faëry ball-floor of her fields in May.
Now her red June sorrel, now her new-turned hay,
Now they keep the great road, now by sheep-path
    stray,
Still it's "England," "England,"
"England" all the way!
Arthur Shearly Cripps.

18. BOLD ROBIN

BOLD Robin has robed him in ghostly attire,
   And forth he is gone like a holy friar,
  Singing, hey down, ho down, down, derry down:
And of two grey friars he soon was aware,
Regaling themselves with dainty fare,
  All on the fallen leaves so brown.

"Good morrow, good brothers," said bold Robin
    Hood,
"And what make you in good greenwood?
  Singing, hey down, ho down, down, derry down:

Now give me, I pray you, wine and food;
For none can I find in the good greenwood,
    All on the fallen leaves so brown."

" Good brother," they said, " we would give you full fain,
But we have no more than enough for twain,
    Singing, hey down, ho down, down, derry down.
" Then give me some money," said bold Robin Hood,
" For none can I find in the good greenwood,
    All on the fallen leaves so brown."

" No money have we, good brother," said they:
" Then," said he, " we three for money will pray,
    Singing, hey down, ho down, down, derry down:
And whatever shall come at the end of our prayer,
We three holy friars shall piously share,
    All on the fallen leaves so brown."

" We will not pray with thee, good brother, God wot;
For truly, good brother, thou pleases us not,
    Singing, hey down, ho down, down, derry down."
Then up they both started from Robin to run,
But down on their knees Robin pulled them each one,
    All on the fallen leaves so brown.

The grey friars prayed with a doleful face,
But bold Robin prayed with a right merry grace,
    Singing, hey down, ho down, down, derry down:
And when they had prayed, their portmanteau he took,
And from it a hundred good angels he shook
    All on the fallen leaves so brown.

"The saints," said bold Robin, "have hearkened our
    prayer,
And here's a good angel apiece for your share;
If more you would have, you must win ere you wear,
    Singing, hey down, ho down, down, derry down."
Then he blew his good horn with a musical cheer,
And fifty green bowmen came trooping full near,
And away the grey friars they bounded like deer,
    All on the fallen leaves so brown.

Thomas Love Peacock.

19. THE WAR-SONG OF DINAS VAWR

THE mountain sheep are sweeter,
    But the valley sheep are fatter;
We therefore deem'd it meeter
To carry off the latter.
We made an expedition;
We met an host and quell'd it;
We forced a strong position,
And kill'd the men who held it.
On Dyfed's richest valley,
Where herds of kine were browsing,
We made a mighty sally,
To furnish our carousing.
Fierce warriors rush'd to meet us;
We met them and o'erthrew them:
They struggled hard to beat us;
But we conquered them, and slew them.
As we drove our prize at leisure,
The king march'd forth to catch us:

His rage surpassed all measure,
But his people could not match us.
He fled to his hall-pillars;
And, ere our force we led off,
Some sack'd his house and cellars,
While others cut his head off.
We there, in strife bewild'ring,
Spilt blood enough to swim in:
We orphan'd many children,
And widow'd many women.
The eagles and the ravens
We glutted with our foemen:
The heroes and the cravens,
The spearmen and the bowmen.
We brought away from battle,
And much their land bemoaned them,
Two thousand head of cattle,
And the head of him who owned them:
Ednyfed, King of Dyfed,
His head was borne before us;
His wine and beasts supplied our feasts,
And his overthrow, our chorus.

Thomas Love Peacock.

20. GOING DOWN HILL ON A BICYCLE
A Boy's Song

With lifted feet, hands still,
I am poised, and down the hill
Dart, with heedful mind;
The air goes by in a wind.

Swifter and yet more swift,
Till the heart, with a mighty lift,
Makes the lungs laugh, the throat cry :—
" O bird! see ; see, bird, I fly.

" Is this, is this your joy,
O bird ? then I, though a boy,
For a golden moment share
Your feathery life in air ! "

Say, heart, is there aught like this
In a world that is full of bliss ?
'Tis more than skating, bound
Steel-shod to the level ground.

Speed slackens now, I float
Awhile in my airy boat ;
Till when the wheels scarce crawl
My feet to the pedals fall.

Alas, that the longest hill
Must end in a vale ; but still,
Who climbs with toil, wheresoe'er,
Shall find wings waiting there.

Henry Charles Beeching.

21. FROM A RAILWAY CARRIAGE

FASTER than fairies, faster than witches,
    Bridges and houses, hedges and ditches ;
And charging along like troops in a battle,
All through the meadows the horses and cattle :

All of the sights of the hill and the plain
Fly as thick as driving rain;
And ever again, in the wink of an eye,
Painted stations whistle by.
Here is a child who clambers and scrambles,
All by himself and gathering brambles;
Here is a tramp who stands and gazes;
And there is the green for stringing the daisies!
Here is a cart run away in the road
Lumping along with man and load;
And here is a mill and there is a river:
Each a glimpse and gone for ever.
Robert Louis Stevenson.

22. TARTARY

If I were Lord of Tartary,
   Myself and me alone,
My bed should be of ivory,
   Of beaten gold my throne;
And in my court would peacocks flaunt,
And in my forests tigers haunt,
And in my pools great fishes slant
   Their fins athwart the sun.

If I were Lord of Tartary,
   Trumpeters every day
To every meal would summon me,
   And in my courtyard bray;
And in the evening lamps should shine,
Yellow as honey, red as wine,
While harp, and flute, and mandoline
   Made music sweet and gay.

If I were Lord of Tartary,
  I'd wear a robe of beads,
White, and gold, and green they'd be—
  And clustered thick as seeds;
And ere should wane the morning star,
I'd don my robe and scimitar,
And zebras seven should draw my car
  Through Tartary's dark glades.

Lord of the fruits of Tartary,
  Her rivers silver-pale!
Lord of the hills of Tartary,
  Glen, thicket, wood, and dale!
Her flashing stars, her scented breeze,
Her trembling lakes, like foamless seas,
Her bird-delighting citron-trees
  In every purple vale!

Walter de la Mare.

23. ROMANCE

When I was but thirteen or so
  I went into a golden land,
Chimborazo, Cotopaxi
  Took me by the hand.

My father died, my brother too,
  They passed like fleeting dreams,
I stood where Popocatapetl
  In the sunlight gleams.

I dimly heard the master's voice
    And boys far-off at play,
Chimborazo, Cotopaxi
    Had stolen me away.

I walked in a great golden dream
    To and fro from school—
Shining Popocatapetl
    The dusty streets did rule.

I walked home with a gold dark boy
    And never a word I'd say,
Chimborazo, Cotopaxi
    Had taken my speech away;

I gazed entranced upon his face
    Fairer than any flower—
O shining Popocatapetl,
    It was thy magic hour:

The houses, people, traffic seemed
    Thin fading dreams by day,
Chimborazo, Cotopaxi
    They had stolen my soul away!

Walter James Turner.

24. OVERHEARD ON A SALTMARSH

Nymph, nymph, what are your beads?
    Green glass, goblin. Why do you stare at them?
Give them me.
        No.

Give them me.   Give them me.
                                No.
Then I will howl all night in the reeds,
Lie in the mud and howl for them.

Goblin, why do you love them so?

They are better than stars or water,
Better than voices of winds that sing,
Better than any man's fair daughter,
Your green beads on a silver ring.

Hush, I stole them out of the moon.

Give me your beads, I desire them.
                                No.
I will howl in a deep lagoon
For your green glass beads, I love them so.
Give them me.   Give them.
                                No.
                        Harold Monro.

25. THE MOCKING FAIRY

"Won't you look out of your window, Mrs. Gill?"
   Quoth the Fairy, nidding, nodding in the garden;
"*Can't* you look out of your window, Mrs. Gill?"
   Quoth the Fairy, laughing softly in the garden;
But the air was still, the cherry boughs were still,
And the ivy-tod 'neath the empty sill,
And never from her window looked out Mrs. Gill
   On the Fairy shrilly mocking in the garden.

"What have they done with you, you poor Mrs.
   Gill?"
Quoth the Fairy, brightly glancing in the garden;
"Where have they hidden you, you poor old Mrs.
   Gill?"
Quoth the Fairy, dancing lightly in the garden;
But night's faint veil now wrapped the hill,
Stark 'neath the stars stood the dead-still Mill,
And out of her cold cottage never answered Mrs. Gill
   The Fairy mimbling mambling in the garden.

Walter de la Mare.

26. THE DEATH OF PUCK

I

I FEAR that Puck is dead—it is so long
   Since men last saw him—dead with all the rest
Of that sweet elfin crew that made their nest
In hollow nuts, where hazels sing their song;
Dead and for ever, like the antique throng
   The elves replaced; the Dryad that you guessed
   Behind the leaves; the Naiad weed-bedressed;
The leaf-eared Faun that loved to lead you wrong.

Tell me, thou hopping Robin, hast thou met
   A little man, no bigger than thyself,
Whom they call Puck, where woodland bells are wet?
Tell me, thou Wood-Mouse, hast thou seen an elf
   Whom they call Puck, and is he seated yet,
Capp'd with a snail-shell, on his mushroom shelf?

II

The Robin gave three hops, and chirped, and said:
  "Yes, I knew Puck, and loved him; though I trow
  He mimicked oft my whistle, chuckling low;
Yes, I knew cousin Puck; but he is dead.
We found him lying on his mushroom bed—
  The Wren and I—half covered up with snow,
  As we were hopping where the berries grow.
We think he died of cold. Ay, Puck is fled."

And then the Wood-Mouse said: "We made the Mole
  Dig him a little grave beneath the moss,
And four big Dormice placed him in the hole.
The Squirrel made with sticks a little cross;
  Puck was a Christian elf, and had a soul;
And all we velvet jackets mourn his loss."

Eugene Lee-Hamilton.

27. THE SHORT CUT TO ROSSES

By the short cut to Rosses a fairy girl I met;
  I was taken in her beauty as a fish is in a net.
The fern uncurled to look at her, so very fair was she,
With her hair as bright as seaweed new-drawn from out the sea.

By the short cut to Rosses ('twas on the first of May)
I heard the fairies piping, and they piped my heart away;

They piped till I was mad with joy, but when I was alone
I found my heart was piped away and in my breast a stone.

By the short cut to Rosses 'tis I'll go never more,
Lest I be robbed of soul by her that stole my heart before,
Lest she take my soul and crush it like a dead leaf in her hand,
For the short cut to Rosses is the way to Fairyland.

Nora Chesson.

28. THE STOLEN CHILD

WHERE dips the rocky highland
Of Sleuth Wood in the lake,
There lies a leafy island
Where flapping herons wake
The drowsy water-rats;
There we've hid our faery vats,
Full of berries,
And of reddest stolen cherries.
Come away, O human child!
To the waters and the wild
With a faery, hand in hand,
For the world's more full of weeping than
 you can understand.

Where the wave of moonlight glosses
The dim grey sands with light,
Far off by furthest Rosses
We foot it all the night,

Weaving olden dances,
Mingling hands and mingling glances
Till the moon has taken flight;
To and fro we leap
And chase the frothy bubbles,
While the world is full of troubles
And is anxious in its sleep.
Come away, O human child!
To the waters and the wild
With a faery, hand in hand,
For the world's more full of weeping than
 you can understand.

Where the wandering water gushes
From the hills above Glen-Car,
In pools among the rushes
That scarce could bathe a star,
We seek for slumbering trout,
And whispering in their ears
Give them unquiet dreams;
Leaning softly out
From ferns that drop their tears
Over the young streams.
Come away, O human child!
To the waters and the wild
With a faery, hand in hand,
For the world's more full of weeping than
 you can understand.

Away with us he's going,
The solemn-eyed:

He'll hear no more the lowing
Of the calves on the warm hillside;
Or the kettle on the hob
Sing peace into his breast,
Or see the brown mice bob
Round and round the oatmeal-chest.
For he comes, the human child,
To the waters and the wild
With a faery, hand in hand,
From a world more full of weeping than
   he can understand.
                    William Butler Yeats.

29. THE FARMER'S BOY

When I went o'er the mountains a farmer's boy to be,
My mother wept all morning when taking leave of me,
My heart was heavy in me, but I thrept that I was gay;
A man of twelve should never weep when going far away.

In the country o'er the mountains the rough roads straggle down,
There's many a long and weary mile 'twixt there and Glenties town;
I went to be a farmer's boy to work the season through,
From Whitsuntide to Hallowe'en, which time the rent came due.

When virgin pure, the dawn's white arm stole o'er
   my mother's door,
From Glenties town I took the road I never trod
   before;
Come Lammas-tide I would not see the trout in
   Greenan's Burn,
And Hallowe'en might come and go, but I would not
   return.

My mother's love for me is warm, her house is cold
   and bare,
A man who wants to see the world has little comfort
   there;
And there 'tis hard to pay the rent, for all you dig
   and delve,
But there's hope beyond the mountains for a little
   man of twelve.

When I went o'er the mountains I worked for days
   on end,
Without a soul to cheer me through or one to call me
   friend;
With older mates I toiled and toiled, in rain and heat
   and wind,
And kept my place. A Glenties man is never left
   behind.

The farmer's wench looked down on me, for she was
   spruce and clean,
But men of twelve don't care for girls like lads of
   seventeen;

And sorrow take the farmer's wench! Her pride
    could never hold
With mine when hoeing turnip fields with fellows
    twice as old.

And so from May to Hallowe'en I wrought and felt
    content,
And sent my wages through the post to pay my
    mother's rent;
For I kept up the Glenties name, and blest, when all
    was done,
The pride that gave a man of twelve the strength of
    twenty-one.

                                    Patrick MacGill.

30. KATE O' BELASHANNY

I

Seek up and down, both fair and brown,
  We've purty lasses many, O;
But brown or fair, one girl most rare,
  The Flow'r o' Belashanny, O.
As straight is she as poplar-tree
  (Tho' not as aisy shaken, O),
And walks so proud among the crowd,
  For queen she might be taken, O.
    From top to toe, where'er you go,
  The loveliest girl of any, O,—
    Ochone! your mind I find unkind,
  Sweet Kate o' Belashanny, O!

II

One summer day the banks were gay,
  The Erne in sunshine glancin' there,
The big cascade its music play'd
  And set the salmon dancin' there.
Along the green my Joy was seen;
  Some goddess bright I thought her there;
The fishes, too, swam close, to view
  Her image in the water there.
    From top to toe, where'er you go,
    The loveliest girl of any, O,—
      Ochone! your mind I find unkind,
    Sweet Kate o' Belashanny, O!

III

My dear, give ear!—the river's near,
  And if you think I'm shammin' now,
To end my grief I'll seek relief
  Among the trout and salmon, now;
For shrimps and sharks to make their marks,
  And other watery vermin there;
Unless a mermaid saves my life,—
  My wife, and me her merman there.
    From top to toe, where'er you go,
    The loveliest girl of any, O,—
      Mavrone! your mind I find unkind,
    Sweet Kate o' Belashanny, O!

IV

'Tis all in vain that I complain;
  No use to coax or chide her there;

As far away from me as Spain,
   Although I stand beside her there.
O cruel Kate ! since that's my fate,
   I'll look for love no more in you ;
The seagull's screech as soon would reach
     Your heart, as me implorin' you.
       Tho' fair you are, and rare you are,
     The loveliest flow'r of any, O,—
       Too proud and high,—good-bye, say I,
To Kate o' Belashanny, O !

                    William Allingham.

31. BIRDS

Sure maybe ye've heard the storm-thrush
   Whistlin' bould in March,
Before there's a primrose peepin' out,
   Or a wee red cone on the larch ;
Whistlin' the sun to come out o' the cloud,
   An' the wind to come over the sea,
But for all he can whistle so clear an' loud,
   He's never the bird for me.

Sure maybe ye've seen the song-thrush
   After an April rain
Slip from in-undher the drippin' leaves,
   Wishful to sing again ;
An' low wi' love when he's near the nest,
   An' loud from the top o' the tree,
But for all he can flutter the heart in your breast,
   He's never the bird for me.

Sure maybe ye've heard the cushadoo
    Callin' his mate in May,
When one sweet thought is the whole of his life,
    An' he tells it the one sweet way.
But my heart is sore at the cushadoo
    Filled wid his own soft glee,
Over an' over his " me an' you ! "
    He's never the bird for me.

Sure maybe ye've heard the red-breast
    Singin' his lone on a thorn,
Mindin' himself o' the dear days lost,
    Brave wid his heart forlorn.
The time is in dark November,
    An' no spring hopes has he :
" Remember," he sings, " remember ! "
    Ay, *thon's* the wee bird for me.

Moira O'Neill.

32. BIRDS OF PARADISE

GOLDEN-winged, silver-winged,
    Winged with flashing flame,
Such a flight of birds I saw,
    Birds without a name :
Singing songs in their own tongue—
    Song of songs—they came.

One to another calling,
    Each answering each,
One to another calling
    In their proper speech :

High above my head they wheeled,
    Far out of reach.

On wings of flame they went and came
    With a cadenced clang:
    Their silver wings tinkled,
    Their golden wings rang;
The wind it whistled through their wings
    Where in heaven they sang.

    They flashed and they darted
        Awhile before mine eyes,
Mounting, mounting, mounting still,
        In haste to scale the skies,
Birds without a nest on earth,
        Birds of Paradise.

    Where the moon riseth not
    Nor sun seeks the west,
    There to sing their glory
    Which they sing at rest,
    There to sing their love-song
    When they sing their best:—

    Not in any garden
        That mortal foot hath trod,
Not in any flowering tree
        That springs from earthly sod,
But in the garden where they dwell,
        The Paradise of God.

Christina Rossetti.

33. CHEATED ELSIE

Elsie was a maiden fair
   As the sun
Shone upon:
Born to teach her swains despair
By smiling on them every one;
Born to win all hearts to her
Just because herself had none;
All the day she had no care,
For she was a maiden fair
As the sun
Shone upon,
Heartless as the brooks that run.

All the maids, with envy tart,
Sneering said, "She has no heart."
All the youths, with bitter smart,
Sighing said, "She has no heart!"
Could she care
For their sneers or their despair
When she was a maiden fair
As the sun
Shone upon,
Heartless as the brooks that run?

But one day whenas she stood
In a wood
Haunted by the fairy brood,
Did she view, or dream she viewed
In a vision's
Wild misprisions,
How a pedlar, dry and rude

As a crook'd branch taking flesh,
Caught the spirit in a mesh,
Singing of—" What is't ye lack ? "
Wizard pack,
On twisted back,
Still he sang, " What is't ye lack ? "

" Lack ye land or lack ye gold,
What I give, I give unsold ;
Lack ye wisdom, lack ye beauty,
To your suit he
Gives unpaid, the pedlar old ! "

Fairies :
    Beware, beware ! the gifts he gives
    One pays for, sweetheart, while one lives.

Elsie :
    What is it the maidens say
    That I lack ?

Pedlar :
    By this bright day
    Can so fair a maiden lack ?
    Maid so sweet
    Should be complete.

Elsie :
    Yet a thing they say I lack.
    In thy pack—
    Pedlar, tell—
    Hast thou ever a heart to sell ?

Pedlar :
    Yea, a heart I have, as tender
    As the mood of evening air.

Elsie:
>Name thy price!

Pedlar:
>The price, by Sorrow!
>Only is, the heart to wear.

Elsie:
>Not great the price, as was my fear.

Fairies:
>So cheap a price was ne'er so dear.
>Beware, beware,
>O rash and fair!
>The gifts he gives,
>Sweetheart, one pays for while one lives!
>
>Scarce the present did she take,
>When the heart began to ache.

Elsie:
>Ah, what is this? Take back thy gift!
>I had not, and I knew no lack;
>Now I have, I lack for ever!

Fairies:
>The gifts he gives, he takes not back.

Elsie:
>Ah, why the present did I take,
>And knew not that a heart would ache?

Fairies:
>Ache! and is that all thy sorrow?—
>Beware, beware,—a heart will break!

>>*Francis Thompson.*

34. THE MAIDS OF ELFIN-MERE

When the spinning-room was here,
    Came Three Damsels, clothed in white,
With their spindles every night;
One and two and three fair Maidens,
Spinning to a pulsing cadence,
Singing songs of Elfin-Mere;
Till the eleventh hour was toll'd,
Then departed through the wold.
    Years ago, and years ago;
    And the tall reeds sigh as the wind doth blow.

Three white Lilies, calm and clear,
And they were loved by everyone;
Most of all, the Pastor's son,
Listening to their gentle singing,
Felt his heart go from him, clinging
To these Maids of Elfin-Mere;
Sued each night to make them stay,
Saddened when they went away.
    Years ago, and years ago;
    And the tall reeds sigh as the wind doth blow.

Hands that shook with love and fear
Dared put back the village clock,—
Flew the spindle, turn'd the rock,
Flow'd the song with subtle rounding,
Till the false " eleven " was sounding;
Then these Maids of Elfin-Mere

Swiftly, softly left the room,
Like three doves on snowy plume.
> *Years ago, and years ago;*
> *And the tall reeds sigh as the wind doth blow.*

One that night who wander'd near
Heard lamentings by the shore,
Saw at dawn three stains of gore
In the waters fade and dwindle.
Never more with song and spindle
Saw we Maids of Elfin-Mere.
The Pastor's son did pine and die;
Because true love should never lie.
> *Years ago, and years ago;*
> *And the tall reeds sigh as the wind doth blow.*
>> *William Allingham.*

35. THE NECKAN

In summer, on the headlands,
    The Baltic Sea along,
Sits Neckan with his harp of gold,
    And sings his plaintive song.

Green rolls beneath the headlands,
    Green rolls the Baltic Sea,
And there, below the Neckan's feet,
    His wife and children be.

He sings not of the ocean,
    Its shells and roses pale.
Of earth, of earth the Neckan sings;
    He hath no other tale.

He sits upon the headlands,
   And sings a mournful stave
Of all he saw and felt on earth,
   Far from the kind sea-wave.

Sings how, a knight, he wander'd
   By castle, field, and town.—
But earthly knights have harder hearts
   Than the sea-children own.

Sings of his earthly bridal—
   Priests, knights, and ladies gay.
—" And who art thou," the priest began,
   " Sir Knight, who wedd'st to-day ? "—

" I am no knight," he answered ;
   " From the sea-waves I come."
The knights drew sword, the ladies scream'd,
   The surpliced priest stood dumb.

He sings how from the chapel
   He vanish'd with his bride,
And bore her down to the sea-halls,
   Beneath the salt sea-tide.

He sings how she sits weeping
   'Mid shells that round her lie.
" False Neckan shares my bed," she weeps ;
   " No Christian mate have I."

He sings how through the billows
   He rose to earth again,
And sought a priest to sign the cross,
   That Neckan Heaven might gain.

He sings how, on an evening,
   Beneath the birch-trees cool,
He sate and play'd his harp of gold,
   Beside the river-pool.

Beside the pool sate Neckan—
   Tears fill'd his mild blue eye.
On his white mule, across the bridge,
   A cassock'd priest rode by.

—" Why sitt'st thou there, O Neckan,
   And play'st thy harp of gold ?
Sooner shall this my staff bear leaves,
   Than thou shalt Heaven behold."—

But, lo, the staff, it budded !
   It green'd, it branch'd, it waved.
—" O ruth of God," the priest cried out,
   " This lost sea-creature saved ! "

The cassock'd priest rode onwards,
   And vanished with his mule;
But Neckan in the twilight grey
   Wept by the river-pool.

He wept : " The earth hath kindness,
   The sea, the starry poles ;
Earth, sea, and sky, and God above—
   But, ah, not human souls ! "

In summer, on the headlands,
   The Baltic Sea along,
Sits Neckan with his harp of gold,
   And sings this plaintive song.

Matthew Arnold.

36. ELDORADO

Gaily bedight,
    A gallant knight,
In sunshine and in shadow,
Had journeyed long,
Singing a song,
In search of Eldorado.

But he grew old—
This knight so bold—
And o'er his heart a shadow
Fell as he found
No spot of ground
That looked like Eldorado.

And, as his strength
Failed him at length,
He met a pilgrim shadow—
"Shadow," said he,
"Where can it be—
This land of Eldorado?"

"Over the Mountains
Of the Moon.
Down the Valley of the Shadow,
Ride, boldly ride,"
The Shade replied,
"If you seek for Eldorado!"

Edgar Allan Poe.

37. THE LUTE-PLAYER

SHE was a lady great and splendid,
  I was a minstrel in her halls.
A warrior like a prince attended
  Stayed his steed by the castle walls.

Far had he fared to gaze upon her.
  " O rest thee now, Sir Knight," she said.
The warrior wooed, the warrior won her,
  In time of snowdrops they were wed.
I made sweet music in his honour,
  And longed to strike him dead.

I passed at midnight from her portal:
  Throughout the world till death I rove:
Ah, let me make this lute immortal
  With rapture of my hate and love!
                            William Watson.

38. TWO RED ROSES ACROSS THE MOON

THERE was a lady lived in a hall,
  Large in the eyes, and slim and tall;
And ever she sung from noon to noon,
Two red roses across the moon.

There was a knight came riding by
In early spring, when the roads were dry;
And he heard that lady sing at the noon,
Two red roses across the moon.

Yet none the more he stopp'd at all,
But he rode a-gallop past the hall;
And left that lady singing at noon,
Two red roses across the moon.

Because, forsooth, the battle was set,
And the scarlet and blue had got to be met,
He rode on the spur till the next warm noon;—
Two red roses across the moon.

But the battle was scatter'd from hill to hill,
From the windmill to the watermill;
And he said to himself, as it near'd the noon,
Two red roses across the moon.

You scarce could see for the scarlet and blue,
A golden helm or a golden shoe:
So he cried, as the fight grew thick at the noon,
Two red roses across the moon!

Verily then the gold bore through
The huddled spears of the scarlet and blue;
And they cried, as they cut them down at the moon,
Two red roses across the moon.

I trow he stopp'd when he rode again
By the hall, though draggled sore with the rain;
And his lips were pinch'd to kiss at the noon
Two red roses across the moon.

Under the may she stoop'd to the crown,
All was gold, there was nothing of brown;
And the horns blew up in the hall at noon,
Two red roses across the moon.

William Morris.

39. LA BELLE DAME SANS MERCI

O WHAT can ail thee, knight-at-arms,
    Alone and palely loitering?
The sedge is wither'd from the lake,
    And no birds sing.

O what can ail thee, knight-at-arms,
    So haggard and so woe-begone?
The squirrel's granary is full,
    And the harvest's done.

I see a lily on thy brow
    With anguish moist and fever dew;
And on thy cheek a fading rose
    Fast withereth too.—

I met a lady in the meads,
    Full beautiful—a faery's child,
Her hair was long, her foot was light,
    And her eyes were wild.

I made a garland for her head,
    And bracelets too, and fragrant zone;
She look'd at me as she did love,
    And made sweet moan.

I set her on my pacing steed,
    And nothing else saw all day long,
For sideways would she lean, and sing
    A faery's song.

She found me roots of relish sweet,
    And honey wild and manna dew,
And sure in language strange she said,
    " I love thee true ! "

She took me to her elfin grot,
    And there she wept and sigh'd full sore,
And there I shut her wild, wild eyes
    With kisses four.

And there she lullèd me asleep,
    And there I dream'd—ah ! woe betide !
The latest dream I ever dream'd
    On the cold hill's side.

I saw pale kings and princes too,
    Pale warriors, death-pale were they all;
They cried—" La Belle Dame sans Merci
    Hath thee in thrall ! "

I saw their starved lips in the gloam
    With horrid warning gapèd wide,
And I awoke and found me here,
    On the cold hill's side.

And this is why I sojourn here,
    Alone and palely loitering,
Though the sedge is wither'd from the lake,
    And no birds sing.

John Keats.

40. THE HAUNTED PALACE

In the greenest of our valleys
    By good angels tenanted,
Once a fair and stately palace—
    Radiant palace—reared its head.
In the monarch Thought's dominion—
    It stood there!
Never seraph spread a pinion
    Over fabric half so fair!

Banners yellow, glorious, golden,
    On its roof did float and flow,
(This—all this—was in the olden
    Time long ago),
And every gentle air that dallied,
    In that sweet day,
Along the ramparts plumed and pallid,
    A wingèd odour went away.

Wanderers in that happy valley,
    Through two luminous windows, saw
Spirits moving musically
    To a lute's well-tunèd law,
Round about a throne where, sitting
    (Porphyrogene!)
In state his glory well befitting,
    The ruler of the realm was seen.

And all with pearl and ruby glowing
    Was the fair palace door,
Through which came flowing, flowing, flowing,
    And sparkling evermore,

A troop of Echoes, whose sweet duty
    Was but to sing,
In voices of surpassing beauty,
    The wit and wisdom of their king.

But evil things, in robes of sorrow,
    Assailed the monarch's high estate.
(Ah! let us mourn!—for never morrow
    Shall dawn upon him desolate!)
And round about his home the glory
    That blushed and bloomed,
Is but a dim-remembered story
    Of the old time entombed.

And travellers, now, within that valley,
    Through the red-litten windows see
Vast forms, that move fantastically
    To a discordant melody,
While, like a ghastly rapid river,
    Through the pale door
A hideous throng rush out for ever,
    And laugh—but smile no more.
Edgar Allan Poe.

41. ANNABEL LEE

It was many and many a year ago,
    In a kingdom by the sea,
That a maiden there lived whom you may know
    By the name of Annabel Lee;
And this maiden she lived with no other thought
    Than to love and be loved by me.

I was a child and *she* was a child,
    In this kingdom by the sea:
But we loved with a love that was more than love—
    I and my Annabel Lee;
With a love that the wingèd seraphs of heaven
    Coveted her and me.

And this was the reason that, long ago,
    In this kingdom by the sea,
A wind blew out of a cloud, chilling
    My beautiful Annabel Lee;
So that her highborn kinsmen came
    And bore her away from me,
To shut her up in a sepulchre
    In this kingdom by the sea.

The angels, not half so happy in heaven,
    Went envying her and me—
Yes!—that was the reason (as all men know,
    In this kingdom by the sea)
That the wind came out of the cloud by night,
    Chilling and killing my Annabel Lee.

But our love it was stronger by far than the love
    Of those who were older than we—
    Of many far wiser than we—
And neither the angels in heaven above,
    Nor the demons down under the sea,
Can ever dissever my soul from the soul
    Of the beautiful Annabel Lee:

For the moon never beams, without bringing me
    dreams
    Of the beautiful Annabel Lee;
And the stars never rise, but I see the bright eyes
    Of the beautiful Annabel Lee;
And so, all the night-tide, I lie down by the side
Of my darling—my darling—my life and my bride,
    In her sepulchre there by the sea,
    In her tomb by the sounding sea.

Edgar Allan Poe.

42. THE TWA SISTERS O' BINNORIE

There were twa sisters sat in a bour,
    Binnorie, O Binnorie!
There came a knight to be their wooer,
    By the bonny mill-dams o' Binnorie.

He courted the eldest wi' glove and ring,
    Binnorie, O Binnorie!
But he lov'd the youngest aboon a' thing,
    By the bonny mill-dams o' Binnorie.

He courted the eldest with broach and knife,
    Binnorie, O Binnorie!
But he lov'd the youngest aboon his life,
    By the bonny mill-dams o' Binnorie.

The eldest she was vexèd sair,
    Binnorie, O Binnorie!
And sair envied her sister fair,
    By the bonny mill-dams o' Binnorie.

The eldest said to the youngest ane,
    Binnorie, O Binnorie!
"Will ye go and see our father's ships come in?"
    By the bonny mill-dams o' Binnorie.

She's ta'en her by the lilly hand,
    Binnorie, O Binnorie!
And led her down to the river strand,
    By the bonny mill-dams o' Binnorie.

The youngest stude upon a stane,
    Binnorie, O Binnorie!
The eldest came and pushed her in,
    By the bonny mill-dams o' Binnorie.

She took her by the middle sma',
    Binnorie, O Binnorie!
And dashed her bonnie back to the jaw,*
    By the bonny mill-dams o' Binnorie.

"O sister, sister, reach your hand!"
    Binnorie, O Binnorie!
"And ye shall be heir of half my land,"
    By the bonny mill-dams o' Binnorie.

"O sister, I'll not reach my hand,"
    Binnorie, O Binnorie!
"And I'll be heir of all your land,"
    By the bonny mill-dams o' Binnorie.

    * Jaw: wave.

"Shame fa' the hand that I should take,"
    Binnorie, O Binnorie!
"It's twin'd me and my world's make,"*
    By the bonny mill-dams o' Binnorie.

"O sister, reach me but your glove,"
    Binnorie, O Binnorie!
"And sweet William shall be your love,"
    By the bonny mill-dams o' Binnorie.

"Sink on, nor hope for hand or glove,"
    Binnorie, O Binnorie!
"And sweet William shall better be my love,"
    By the bonny mill-dams o' Binnorie.

"Your cherry cheeks and your yellow hair,"
    Binnorie, O Binnorie!
"Garr'd me gang maiden evermair,"
    By the bonny mill-dams o' Binnorie.

Sometimes she sunk, and sometimes she swam,
    Binnorie, O Binnorie!
Until she came to the miller's dam,
    By the bonny mill-dams o' Binnorie!

"O father, father, draw your dam!"
    Binnorie, O Binnorie!
"There's either a mermaid or a milk-white swan,"
    By the bonny mill-dams o' Binnorie.

* World's make: earthly mate.

The miller hasted and drew his dam,
    Binnorie, O Binnorie!
And there he found a drowned woman,
    By the bonny mill-dams o' Binnorie.

You could not see her yellow hair,
    Binnorie, O Binnorie!
For gowd and pearls that were sae rare,
    By the bonny mill-dams o' Binnorie.

You could na' see her middle sma',
    Binnorie, O Binnorie!
Her gowden girdle was sae bra',
    By the bonny mill-dams o' Binnorie.

An' by there came a harper fine,
    Binnorie, O Binnorie!
That harpèd to the king at dine,
    By the bonny mill-dams o' Binnorie.

When he did look that lady upon,
    Binnorie, O Binnorie!
He sigh'd and made a heavy moan,
    By the bonny mill-dams o' Binnorie.

He's ta'en three locks o' her yallow hair,
    Binnorie, O Binnorie!
And wi' them strung his harp sae fair,
    By the bonny mill-dams o' Binnorie.

The first tune he did play and sing,
    Binnorie, O Binnorie!
Was, "Farewell to my father the king,"
    By the bonny mill-dams o' Binnorie.

The nextin tune that he played syne,
    Binnorie, O Binnorie !
Was, " Farewell to my mother the queen,"
    By the bonny mill-dams o' Binnorie.

The lasten tune that he played then,
    Binnorie, O Binnorie !
Was " Wae to my sister, fair Ellen ! "
    By the bonny mill-dams o' Binnorie.
                   Old Ballad.

43. FAIR HELEN OF KIRCONNEL

I wish I were where Helen lies,
    Night and day on me she cries;
Oh, that I were where Helen lies,
    On fair Kirconnel lea !
Oh, Helen fair, beyond compare,
I'll mak' a garland o' thy hair,
Shall bind my heart for ever mair,
    Until the day I dee.

Oh, think na ye my heart was sair,
When my love dropped down and spak nae mair !
She sank, and swoon'd wi mickle care,
    On fair Kirconnel lea.
Curst be the heart that thought the thought,
And curst the hand that shot the shot,
When in my arms burd * Helen dropt,
    And died to succour me.

* Burd: maiden.

As I went down the water-side,
None but my foe to be my guide,
None but my foe to be my guide,
    On fair Kirconnel lea,
I lighted down, my sword did draw,
I hackèd him in pieces sma',
I hackèd him in pieces sma',
    For her sake that died for me.

Oh, that I were where Helen lies!
Night and day on me she cries,
Out of my bed she bids me rise—
    "Oh come, my love, to me!"
Oh, Helen fair! Oh, Helen chaste!
If I were with thee I were blest,
Where thou lies low and takes thy rest,
    On fair Kirconnel lea.

I wish my grave were growin' green,
A windin' sheet drawn o'er my een,
And I in Helen's arms lying,
    On fair Kirconnel lea.
I wish I were where Helen lies,
Night and day on me she cries;
And I am weary of the skies,
    For her sake that died for me.
                  Old Ballad.

44. LORD RANDAL

"O WHERE have ye been, Lord Randal, my son?
    O where have ye been, my handsome young man?"

"I have been to the wild wood; mother, make my
  bed soon,
For I'm weary wi' hunting, and fain would lie down."

"Where gat ye your dinner, Lord Randal, my son?
Where gat ye your dinner, my handsome young
  man?"
"I din'd wi' my true-love; mother, make my bed
  soon,
For I'm weary wi' hunting, and fain would lie down."

"What gat ye to your dinner, Lord Randal, my son?
What gat ye to your dinner, my handsome young
  man?"
"I gat eels boiled in broo'; mother, make my bed
  soon,
For I'm weary wi' hunting, and fain would lie down."

"What became of your bloodhounds, Lord Randal,
  my son?
What became of your bloodhounds, my handsome
  young man?"
"O they swell'd and they died; mother, make my
  bed soon,
For I'm weary wi' hunting, and fain would lie down."

"O I fear ye are poison'd, Lord Randal, my son!
O I fear ye are poison'd, my handsome young man!"
"O yes, I am poison'd; mother, make my bed soon,
For I'm sick at the heart, and I fain would lie down."

Old Ballad.

45. LENORE

Ah, broken is the golden bowl! the spirit flown
    for ever!
Let the bell toll!—a saintly soul floats on the Stygian
    river.
And, Guy de Vere, hast *thou* no tear? weep now or
    never more!
See! on yon drear and rigid bier low lies thy love,
    Lenore!
Come! let the burial rite be read—the funeral song
    be sung!—
An anthem for the queenliest dead that ever died so
    young—
A dirge for her, the doubly dead in that she died so
    young.

Wretches! ye loved her for her wealth and hated
    her for her pride,
And when she fell in feeble health, ye blessed her—
    that she died!
How *shall* the ritual, then, be read?—the requiem
    how be sung
By you—by yours, the evil eye,—by yours, the slan-
    derous tongue
That did to death the innocence that died, and died
    so young?

Peccavimus; but rave not thus! and let a Sabbath
    song
Go up to God so solemnly the dead may feel no
    wrong!

The sweet Lenore hath gone before, with Hope, that
    flew beside,
Leaving thee wild for the dear child that should have
    been thy bride—
For her, the fair and débonnaire, that now so lowly
    lies,
The life upon her yellow hair but not within her eyes—
The life still there, upon her hair—the death upon
    her eyes.

Avaunt! to-night my heart is light. No dirge will I
    upraise,
But waft the angel on her flight with a pæan of old
    days!
Let *no* bell toll!—lest her sweet soul, amid its hal-
    lowed mirth,
Should catch the note, as it doth float up from the
    damnèd Earth.
To friends above, from fiends below, the indignant
    ghost is riven—
From Hell unto a high estate far up within the
    Heaven—
From grief and groan to a golden throne beside the
    King of Heaven.

Edgar Allan Poe.

46. PERSEPHONE

I

She stepped upon Sicilian grass,
   Demeter's daughter, fresh and fair;
A child of light, a radiant lass,
   And gamesome as the morning air.
The daffodils were fair to see,
They nodded lightly on the lea,
Persephone—Persephone!

Lo! one she marked of rarer growth
   Than orchis or anemone;
For it the maiden left them both,
   And parted from her company.
Drawn nigh she deemed it fairer still,
And stooped to gather by the rill
The daffodil, the daffodil.

What ailed the meadow that it shook?
   What ailed the air of Sicily?
She wandered by the brattling brook,
   And trembled with the trembling lea.
"The coal-black horses rise—they rise:
O Mother, Mother!" low she cries—
Persephone—Persephone!

"O light, light, light!" she cries, "farewell;
   The coal-black horses wait for me.
O shades of shades, where I must dwell.
   Demeter, Mother, far from thee!

Ah, fated doom that I fulfil !
Ah, fateful flower beside the rill !
The daffodil, the daffodil ! "

What ails her that she comes not home ?
    Demeter seeks her far and wide,
And gloomy-browed doth ceaseless roam
    From many a morn till eventide.
" My life, immortal though it be,
Is nought," she cries, " for want of thee,
Persephone—Persephone !

" Meadows of Enna, let the rain
    No longer drop to feed your rills,
Nor deep refresh the fields again,
    With all their nodding daffodils !
Fade, fade and droop, O lilied lea,
Where thou, dear heart, wast reft from me—
Persephone—Persephone ! "

II

She reigns upon her dusky throne,
    'Mid shades of heroes dread to see ;
Among the dead she breathes alone,
    Persephone—Persephone !
Or seated on the Elysian hill
She dreams of earthly daylight still,
And murmurs of the daffodil.

A voice in Hades soundeth clear,
  The shadows mourn and flit below;
It cries—"Thou Lord of Hades, hear,
  And let Demeter's daughter go.
The tender corn upon the lea
Droops in her golden gloom when she
Cries for her lost Persephone.

"From land to land she raging flies,
  The green fruit falleth in her wake,
And harvest fields beneath her eyes
  To earth the grain unripened shake.
Arise and set the maiden free;
Why should the world such sorrows dree
By reason of Persephone?"

He takes the cleft pomegranate seeds,
  "Love, eat with me this parting day;"
Then bids them fetch the coal-black steeds—
  Demeter's daughter, would'st away?
The gates of Hades set her free,
"She will return full soon," saith he—
"My wife, my wife Persephone."

Low laughs the dark king on his throne—
  "I gave her of pomegranate seeds;"
Demeter's daughter stands alone
  Upon the fair Elysian meads.
Her mother meets her. "Hail!" saith she;
"And doth our daylight dazzle thee,
My love, my child, Persephone!

"What moved thee, daughter, to forsake
  Thy fellow maids that fatal morn,
And give thy dark lord power to take
  Thee living to his realm forlorn?"
Her lips reply without her will,
As one addressed who slumbereth still—
"The daffodil, the daffodil!"

Her eyelids droop with light oppressed,
  And sunny wafts around her stir,
Her cheek is on her mother's breast,
  Demeter's kisses comfort her.
Calm queen of Hades, art thou she
Who stepped so lightly on the lea—
Persephone, Persephone?

    .   .   .   .   .

Demeter sighs, but sure 'tis well
  The wife should love her destiny;
They part, and yet, as legends tell,
  She mourns her lost Persephone;
While chant the maids of Enna still—
"O fateful flower beside the rill—
The daffodil, the daffodil!"
Jean Ingelow.

47. THE BOY AND THE ANGEL

Morning, evening, noon and night,
  "Praise God!" sang Theocrite.

Then to his poor trade he turned,
Whereby the daily meal was earned.

Hard he laboured, long and well;
O'er his work the boy's curls fell.

But ever, at each period,
He stopped and sang, " Praise God ! "

Then back again his curls he threw,
And cheerful turned to work anew.

Said Blaise, the listening monk, " Well done;
I doubt not thou art heard, my son:

" As well as if thy voice to-day
Were praising God, the Pope's great way.

" This Easter Day, the Pope at Rome
Praises God from Peter's dome."

Said Theocrite, " Would God that I
Might praise Him, that great way, and die ! "

Night passed, day shone,
And Theocrite was gone.

With God a day endures alway,
A thousand years are but a day.

God said in heaven, " Nor day nor night
Now brings the voice of my delight."

Then Gabriel, like a rainbow's birth,
Spread his wings and sank to earth:

Entered, in flesh, the empty cell,
Lived there, and played the craftsman well;

And morning, evening, noon and night,
Praised God in place of Theocrite.

And from a boy, to youth he grew:
The man put off the stripling's hue:

The man matured and fell away
Into the season of decay:

And ever o'er the trade he bent,
And ever lived on earth content.

(He did God's will; to him, all one
If on the earth or in the sun.)

God said, " A praise is in mine ear;
There is no doubt in it, no fear:

" So sing old worlds, and so
New worlds that from my footstool go.

" Clearer loves sound other ways:
I miss my little human praise."

Then forth sprang Gabriel's wings, off fell
The flesh disguise, remained the cell.

'Twas Easter Day: he flew to Rome,
And paused above Saint Peter's dome.

In the tiring-room close by
The great outer gallery,

With his holy vestments dight,
Stood the new Pope, Theocrite:

And all his past career
Came back upon him clear,

Since when, a boy, he plied his trade,
Till on his life the sickness weighed;

And in his cell, when death drew near,
An angel in a dream brought cheer:

And rising from the sickness drear
He grew a priest, and now stood here.

To the East with praise he turned,
And on his sight the angel burned.

" I bore thee from thy craftsman's cell
And set thee here; I did not well.

" Vainly I left my angel-sphere,
Vain was thy dream of many a year.

" Thy voice's praise seemed weak; it dropped—
Creation's chorus stopped!

" Go back and praise again
The early way, while I remain.

"With that weak voice of our disdain,
Take up creation's pausing strain.

" Back to the cell and poor employ :
Resume the craftsman and the boy ! "

Theocrite grew old at home ;
A new Pope dwelt in Peter's dome.

One vanished as the other died :
They sought God side by side.
Robert Browning.

48. A BALLAD OF ST. CHRISTOPHER

There dwelt at the court of a good king
   A giant huge and black,
He could take up Gedney Church
   And carry it on his back ;
A giant fierce and grim as he
No king had in his giantry.

This paynim wight was dull of wit,
   But he held fast one thing,
That the strongest man in all the world
   Should serve the strongest king,
A purpose firm he had in mind,
The mightiest king on earth to find.

A minstrel sang a song of the Devil,
The giant gasped to see
That the king made at the Devil's name
A sign with fingers three.
"Ho! ho!" said the giant, "I stay not here
To serve a king who goes in fear."

The giant found the great black Devil,
And did him homage true,
To be his faithful bondservant,
His bidding aye to do;
With his new master night and morn
He fired farmsteads and trampled corn.

They went on a lonely road one day,
Plotting great harm and loss;
"I must turn back," the Devil said sudden,
"For here I see a Cross."
"Ho! ho!" said the giant, "is here the sign
Of a king whose power is more than thine?"

"Gallows of God!" the Devil said,
And white with rage went he,
"He took the gallows for Himself,
That, sure, belonged to me;
He took the gallows, He took the thief,
He stole my harvest sheaf by sheaf.

"He broke my gates, He harried my realm,
He freed my prisoned folk,
He crowned His Mother for Eve discrowned,
My kingdom went like smoke;

Where'er I go by night or day
That sign has power to bar my way.

" Great is my might, but against the clan
Of this King I have no charm ;
If they touch water, if they touch wood,
I cannot work them harm ;
I go a wanderer without rest
Where fingers three touch brow and breast ! "

" God keep thee, Devil," the giant said,
" Thy riddle I cannot read,
But from thy company here and now
I must depart with speed ;
I hold thee but as a beaten knave,
To find that mightiest King I crave."

The giant came to an old, old man
That worked among his bees,
He gathered wax for the altar lights
In white beneath green trees ;
The sun shone through him and he, too, shone,
For he was the Blessèd Apostle John.

He asked the old man of that king,
Whose bondslave he would be,
" Thro' wood," said St. John, " there is healing in water,
His servants all are free,"
He christened him and straightway then
Told of the tasks of christened men.

"Some wear the stone with their bent knees,
Some holy pictures limn,
Some bear the news of Christ to lands
That have not heard of Him."
The giant said, "If I had the will
For this, I have no wit nor skill."

"To ford," St. John said, "yonder river,
Poor wayfarers essay,
And by the great swiftness of the stream
Many are swept away;
Who carries them over will do a thing
To pleasure greatly the Strong King."

The giant came to that wild water,
And on its brink did dwell,
He saved the lives of wayfarers
More than a man may tell;
And there it chanced one midnight wild
He heard the cry of a little child.

The child held a globe in his hand,
He begged to cross that night;
The giant set him on his shoulder
As a burden sweet and light;
Into the stream with a careless laugh
He stepped with a palm tree for a staff.

But the child grew heavier and his globe
Until they weighed like lead,
"Deus meus et omnia,
What child is this?" he said:

It seemed as the waves swelled and whirled
He felt the weight of all the world.

Sure, all the churches upon earth
He bore with tottering feet,
Rouen, Amiens, Bourges and Chartres,
Long Sutton, Gedney, Fleet;
So sweet, so terrible the load,
It was as though he carried God.

The bells of all those churches rang
When they had gained the shore,
He saw no child, but a great King
Of might unguessed before;
The King on Whom the world is stayed,
That is the Son of the pure Maid.

"I thank thee, Christopher, that thou
So well hast kept My rule;
Thou hast borne Me with Heaven My throne
And the earth My footstool."
He felt strange joy within him stir
As the King called him "Christopher."

On fair days and on market-days,
Where men to fiddles sing,
They tell of the strongest man on earth
Who served the mightiest King.
For that great King he served so well,
He loves the song and the fiddél.

Richard Lawson Gales.

49. ST. GEORGE AND THE DRAGON

A Cornish Christmas Play

Characters

Saint George　　　　　　　The Doctor
The Dragon　　　　　　　 King of Egypt
Father Christmas　　　　　Turkish Knight
　　　　　The Giant Turpin

Enter the Turkish Knight.

Open your doors, and let me in,
　I hope your favours I shall win;
Whether I rise or whether I fall,
I'll do my best to please you all.
St. George is here, and swears he will come in,
And, if he does, I know he'll pierce my skin.
If you will not believe what I do say,
Let Father Christmas come in—clear the way.
　　　　　　　　　　　　　(*Retires.*)

Enter Father Christmas.

Here come I, old Father Christmas,
　Welcome, or welcome not,
I hope old Father Christmas
　Will never be forgot.

I am not come here to laugh or to jeer,
But for a pocketfull of money and a skinfull of beer,
If you will not believe what I do say,
Come in, the King of Egypt!—clear the way!

Enter the King of Egypt.

Here I, the King of Egypt, boldly do appear,
St. George, St. George, walk in, my only son and heir.

Walk in, my son, St. George, and boldly act thy part,
That all the people here may see thy wond'rous art.

Enter St. George.

Here come I, St. George, from Britain did I spring,
I'll fight the Dragon bold, my wonders to begin.
I'll clip his wings, he shall not fly;
I'll cut him down or else I die.

Enter the Dragon.

Who's he that seeks the Dragon's blood,
And calls so angry, and so loud?
That English dog, will he before me stand?
I'll cut him down with my courageous hand.
With my long teeth and scurvy jaw,
Of such I'd break up half a score,
And stay my stomach, till I'd more.

(St. George *and the* Dragon *fight; the latter is killed.*)

Father Christmas:

Is there a doctor to be found
   All ready, near at hand,
To cure a deep and deadly wound,
   And make the champion stand.

Enter Doctor.

Oh! yes, there is a doctor to be found
   All ready, near at hand,
To cure a deep and deadly wound,
   And make the champion stand.

Father Christmas:
What can you cure?

Doctor:
All sorts of diseases,
Whatever you pleases,
The phthisic, the palsy, and the gout;
If the devil's in, I'll blow him out.

Father Christmas:
What is your fee?

Doctor:
Fifteen pound, it is my fee,
   The money to lay down.
But, as 'tis such a rogue as thee,
   I cure for ten pound.

I carry a little bottle of alicumpane;
   Here, Jack, take a little of my flip flop,
   Pour it down thy tip top;
Rise up and fight again.

      (*The* DOCTOR *performs his cure, the fight is renewed and the* DRAGON *again killed.*)

Saint George:
Here am I, St. George,
   That worthy champion bold,
And with my sword and spear
   I won three crowns of gold.

I fought the fiery dragon,
  And brought him to the slaughter;
By that I won fair Sabra,
  The King of Egypt's daughter.
Where is the man that now will me defy?
I'll cut his giblets full of holes, and make his buttons
    fly.

The TURKISH KNIGHT *advances.*

Here come I, the Turkish Knight,
Come from the Turkish land to fight.
I'll fight St. George, who is my foe,
I'll make him yield before I go;
He brags to such a high degree,
He thinks there's none can do the like of he.

Saint George:

Where is the Turk that will before me stand?
I'll cut him down with my courageous hand.

> (*They fight, the* KNIGHT *is overcome and falls on one knee.*)

Turkish Knight:

Oh! pardon me, St. George, pardon of thee I crave,
Oh! pardon me this night, and I will be thy slave.

Saint George:

No pardon shalt thou have, while I have foot to stand,
So rise thee up again, and fight out sword in hand.

> (*They fight again and the* KNIGHT *is killed.* FATHER CHRISTMAS *calls for the* DOCTOR, *with whom the same dialogue occurs as before, and the cure is performed.*)

Enter the GIANT TURPIN.

Here come I, the Giant, bold Turpin is my name,
And all the nations round do tremble at my fame.
Where'er I go, they tremble at my sight,
No lord or champion long with me would fight.

Saint George:

Here's one that dares to look thee in the face,
And soon will send thee to another place.

> (*They fight, and the* GIANT *is killed; medical aid is called in as before, and the cure performed by the* DOCTOR, *to whom then is given a basin of girdy grout and a kick and he is driven out.*)

Father Christmas:

Now, ladies and gentlemen, your sport is most ended,
So prepare for the hat, which is highly commended.
The hat it would speak, if it had but a tongue,
Come, throw in your money, and think it no wrong.

END OF PART I

THE
DAFFODIL POETRY BOOK

PART II

50. JANUARY DUSK

Austere and clad in sombre robes of grey,
   With hands upfolded and with silent wings,
In unimpassioned mystery the day
   Passes; a lonely thrush its requiem sings.

The dust of night is tangled in the boughs
   Of leafless lime and lilac, and the pine
Grows blacker, and the star upon the brows
   Of sleep is set in heaven for a sign.

Earth's little weary peoples fall on peace
   And dream of breaking buds and blossoming,
Of primrose airs, of days of large increase,
   And all the coloured retinue of spring.

John Drinkwater.

51. SONG

All suddenly the wind comes soft
   And Spring is here again;
And the hawthorn quickens with buds of green,
   And my heart with buds of pain.

My heart all Winter lay so numb,
   The earth so dead and frore,
That I never thought the Spring would come,
   Or my heart wake any more.

But Winter's broken and earth has woken,
   And the small birds cry again;
And the hawthorn hedge puts forth its buds,
   And my heart puts forth its pain.

Rupert Brooke.

52. TO SPRING

O THOU with dewy locks, who lookest down
   Through the clear windows of the morning, turn
Thine angel eyes upon our western isle,
Which in full choir hails thy approach, O Spring!

The hills tell each other, and the listening
Valleys hear; all our longing eyes are turned
Up to thy bright pavilions: issue forth,
And let thy holy feet visit our clime!

Come o'er the eastern hills, and let our winds
Kiss thy perfumèd garments; let us taste
Thy morn and evening breath; scatter thy pearls
Upon our lovesick land that mourns for thee.

Oh, deck her forth with thy fair fingers; pour
Thy soft kisses on her bosom; and put
Thy golden crown upon her languished head,
Whose modest tresses were bound up for thee!

William Blake.

53. RONDEAU

ON Newlyn Hill the gorse is bright;
    Upon the hedgerows left and right
Song-dizzy birds the Spring-time greet;
The bluebells weave a purple sheet;
Primroses star the lanes' green night.

Across the Bay each moorland height
Glows golden in the evening light,
And Dusk walks violet-eyed and sweet
    On Newlyn Hill.

A swarm of lights, pearl-soft and white,
A fairy-lamp-land exquisite,
Opens its star-eyes at the feet
Of hills where shore and wavelets meet;
Then dreams come, mystic, infinite,
    On Newlyn Hill.

Crosbie Garstin.

54. BUDS

THE raining hour is done,
    And, threaded on the bough,
The may-buds in the sun
    Are shining emeralds now.

As transitory these
    As things of April will,
Yet, trembling in the trees,
    Is briefer beauty still.

For, flowering from the sky
  Upon an April day,
Are silver buds that lie
  Amid the buds of may.

The April emeralds now,
  While thrushes fill the lane,
Are linked along the bough
  With silver buds of rain.

And, straightly though to earth
  The buds of silver slip,
The green buds keep the mirth
  Of that companionship.

John Drinkwater.

55. THE PINKS

The pinks along my garden walks
  Have all shot forth their summer stalks,
Thronging their buds 'mong tulips hot,
  And blue forget-me-not.

Their dazzling snows forth-bursting soon
Will lade the idle breath of June;
And waken thro' the fragrant night
  To steal the pale moonlight.

The nightingale at end of May
Lingers each year for their display;
Till when he sees their blossoms blown,
  He knows the spring is flown.

June's birth they greet, and when their bloom
Dislustres, withering on his tomb,
Then summer hath a shortening day;
    And steps slow to decay.

Robert Bridges.

56. NORTH WIND IN OCTOBER

IN the golden glade the chestnuts are fallen all;
    From the sered boughs of the oak the acorns fall:
The beech scatters her ruddy fire;
The lime hath stripped to the cold,
And standeth naked above her yellow attire:
The larch thinneth her spire
To lay the ways of the wood with cloth of gold.

Out of the golden-green and white
Of the brake the fir-trees stand upright
In the forest of flame, and wave aloft
To the blue of heaven their blue-green tuftings soft.

But swiftly in shuddering gloom the splendours fail,
As the harrying North-wind beareth
A cloud of skirmishing hail
The grievèd woodland to smite:
In a hurricane through the trees he teareth,
Raking the boughs and the leaves rending,
And whistleth to the descending
Blows of his icy flail.
Gold and snow he mixeth in spite,
And whirleth afar; as away on his winnowing flight
He passeth, and all again for awhile is bright.

Robert Bridges.

57. TO A SNOWFLAKE

What heart could have thought you ?—
    Past our devisal
(O filigree petal !)
Fashioned so purely,
Fragilely, surely,
From what Paradisal
Imagineless metal,
Too costly for cost ?
Who hammered you, wrought you,
From argentine vapour ?—
" God was my shaper.
Passing surmisal,
He hammered, He wrought me,
From curled silver vapour,
To lust of His mind :—
Thou couldst not have thought me !
So purely, so palely,
Tinily, surely,
Mightily, frailly,
Insculped and embossed,
With His hammer of wind,
And His graver of frost."

Francis Thompson.

58. CAROL

Outlanders, whence come ye last ?
    The snow in the street and the wind on the door.
Through what green seas and great have ye passed ?
    Minstrels and maids, stand forth on the floor.

From far away, O masters mine,
  The snow in the street and the wind on the door.
We come to bear you goodly wine.
  Minstrels and maids, stand forth on the floor.

From far away we come to you,
  The snow in the street and the wind on the door.
To tell of great tidings strange and true.
  Minstrels and maids, stand forth on the floor.

News, news of the Trinity,
  The snow in the street and the wind on the door.
And Mary and Joseph from over the sea!
  Minstrels and maids, stand forth on the floor.

For as we wandered far and wide,
  The snow in the street and the wind on the door.
What hap do ye deem there should us betide?
  Minstrels and maids, stand forth on the floor.

Under a bent when the night was deep,
  The snow in the street and the wind on the door.
There lay three shepherds tending their sheep.
  Minstrels and maids, stand forth on the floor.

"O ye shepherds, what have ye seen,
  The snow in the street and the wind on the door.
To slay your sorrow, and heal your teen?"
  Minstrels and maids, stand forth on the floor

"In an ox-stall this night we saw,
  The snow in the street and the wind on the door.
A babe and a maid without a flaw.
  Minstrels and maids, stand forth on the floor.

"There was an old man there beside,
  The snow in the street and the wind on the door.
His hair was white and his hood was wide.
  Minstrels and maids, stand forth on the floor.

"And as we gazed this thing upon,
  The snow in the street and the wind on the door.
Those twain knelt down to the Little One.
  Minstrels and maids, stand forth on the floor.

"And a marvellous song we straight did hear,
  The snow in the street and the wind on the door.
That slew our sorrow and healed our care,"
  Minstrels and maids, stand forth on the floor.

News of a fair and a marvellous thing,
  The snow in the street and the wind on the door.
Nowell, nowell, nowell, we sing!
  Minstrels and maids, stand forth on the floor.

William Morris.

59. A CHRISTMAS LEGEND

Abroad on a winter's night there ran
  Under the starlight, leaping the rills
Swollen with snow-drip from the hills,
  Goat-legged, goat-bearded Pan.

He loved to run on the crisp white floor,
Where black hill-torrents chiselled grooves,
And he loved to print his clean-cut hooves,
  Where none had trod before.

And now he slacked and came to a stand
Beside a river too broad to leap;
And as he panted he heard a sheep
    That bleated near at hand.

" Bell-wether, bell-wether, what do you say ?
Peace, and huddle your ewes from cold ! "
" Master, but ere we went to fold
    Our herdsman hastened away:

"Over the hill came other twain
And pointed away to Bethlehem,
And spake with him, and he followed them,
    And has not come again.

" He dropped his pipe of the river-reed;
He left his scrip in his haste to go;
And all our grazing is under snow,
    So that we cannot feed."

" Left his sheep on a winter's night ? "—
Pan folded them with an angry frown.
" Bell-wether, bell-wether, I'll go down
    Where the star shines bright."

Down by the hamlet he met the man.
" Shepherd, no shepherd, thy flock is lorn ! "
" Master, no master, a child is born
    Royal, greater than Pan.

" Lo, I have seen; I go to my sheep;
Follow my footsteps through the snow,
But warily, warily see thou go,
    For child and mother sleep."

Into the stable-yard Pan crept,
And there in a manger a baby lay
Beside his mother upon the hay,
   And mother and baby slept.

Pan bent over the sleeping child,
Gazed on him, panting after his run:
And while he wondered, the little one
   Opened his eyes and smiled;

Smiled, and after a little space
Struggled an arm from the swaddling-band,
And raising a tiny dimpled hand,
   Patted the bearded face.

Something snapped in the breast of Pan;
His heart, his throat, his eyes were sore,
And he wished to weep as never before
   Since the world began.

And out he went to the silly sheep,
To the fox on the hill, the fish in the sea,
The horse in the stall, the bird in the tree,
   Asking them how to weep.

They could not teach—they did not know;
The law stands writ for the beast that's dumb
That a limb may ache and a heart be numb,
   But never a tear can flow.

So bear you kindly to-day, O Man,
To all that is dumb and all that is wild,
For the sake of the Christmas Babe who smiled
   In the eyes of great god Pan.

Frank Sidgwick.

60. AN ODE OF THE BIRTH OF OUR SAVIOUR

In numbers, and but these few,
    I sing Thy birth, O Jesu!
Thou pretty baby, born here,
With sup'rabundant scorn here;
Who for Thy princely port here,
    Hadst for Thy place
    Of birth a base
Out-stable for Thy court here.

Instead of neat enclosures
Of interwoven osiers,
Instead of fragrant posies
Of daffodils and roses,
Thy cradle, Kingly Stranger,
    As Gospel tells,
    Was nothing else
But here a homely manger.

But we with silks, not crewels,
With sundry precious jewels,
And lily-work will dress Thee;
And as we dispossess Thee
Of clouts, we'll make a chamber,
    Sweet babe, for Thee
    Of ivory,
And plaister'd round with amber.

The Jews they did disdain Thee,
But we will entertain Thee,
With glories to await here,
Upon Thy princely state here;
And more for love than pity,
    From year to year,
    We'll make Thee, here,
A freeborn of our city.

Robert Herrick.

61. TO MORNING

O HOLY virgin, clad in purest white,
    Unlock heaven's golden gates, and issue forth;
Awake the dawn that sleeps in heaven; let light
Rise from the chambers of the East, and bring
The honeyed dew that cometh on waking day.
O radiant Morning, salute the Sun,
Roused like a huntsman to the chase, and with
Thy buskined feet appear upon our hills.

William Blake.

62. "DAY" (FROM "PIPPA PASSES")

Day!
    Faster and more fast,
O'er night's brim, day boils at last;
Boils, pure gold, o'er the cloud-cup's brim
Where spurting and suppressed it lay,
For not a froth-flake touched the rim
Of yonder gap in the solid gray
Of the eastern cloud, an hour away;

But forth one wavelet, then another, curled,
Till the whole sunrise, not to be suppressed,
Rose, reddened, and its seething breast
Flickered in bounds, grew gold, then overflowed the world.

Robert Browning.

63. TO NIGHT

Swiftly walk over the western wave,
    Spirit of Night!
Out of the misty eastern cave,
Where, all the long and lone daylight,
Thou wovest dreams of joy and fear,
Which make thee terrible and dear,—
    Swift be thy flight!

Wrap thy form in a mantle gray,
    Star-inwrought!
Blind with thine hair the eyes of Day,
Kiss her until she be wearied out,
Then wander o'er city, and sea, and land,
Touching all with thine opiate wand—
    Come, long sought!

When I arose and saw the dawn,
    I sighed for thee;
When light rode high, and the dew was gone,
And noon lay heavy on flower and tree,
And the weary Day turned to his rest,
Lingering like an unloved guest
    I sighed for thee.

Thy brother Death came, and cried,
    Would'st thou me ?
Thy sweet child Sleep, the filmy-eyed,
Murmured like a noontide bee,
Shall I nestle near thy side ?
Would'st thou me ?—And I replied,
    No, not thee !

Death will come when thou art dead,
    Soon, too soon—
Sleep will come when thou art fled ;
Of neither would I ask the boon
I ask of thee, belovèd Night—
Swift be thine approaching flight,
    Come soon, soon !

Percy Bysshe Shelley.

64. DONNYBROOK

I saw the moon so broad and bright
  Sailing high on a frosty night :

And the air swung far and far between
The silver disc and the orb of green :

While here and there a wisp of white
Cloud-film swam on the misty light :

And crusted thickly on the sky,
High and higher and yet more high,

Were golden star-points dusted through
The great, wide, silent vault of blue

Then I said to me —God is good
And the world is fair—and where I stood

I knelt me down and bent my head,
And said my prayers, and went to bed.
>> *James Stephens.*

65. SLEEP

A FLOCK of sheep that leisurely pass by,
  One after one ; the sound of rain, and bees
Murmuring ; the fall of rivers, winds, and seas,
Smooth fields, white sheets of water, and pure sky ;
I have thought of all by turns, and yet do lie
Sleepless ! and soon the small birds' melodies
Must hear, first uttered from my orchard trees ;
And the first cuckoo's melancholy cry.
Even thus last night, and two nights more, I lay
And could not win thee, Sleep ! by any stealth :
So do not let me wear to-night away :
Without thee what is all the morning's wealth ?
Come, blessed barrier between day and day,
Dear mother of fresh thoughts and joyous health !
>> *William Wordsworth.*

66. PHOSPHORESCENCE

I WENT into the larder,
  In a mood like dark night—
The cold little larder
  Without a gleam of light.

Overhead, the moon's crescent
Amber-gold, opalescent,
Herded slow, acquiescent
Flocks of sheep, fleecy white.

As I glanced idly, giving
    A swing to the door,
Something flashed at me, living,
    Like eyes in the floor:
        Something wrought of sheer moonlight,
        Blue and green and silver-bright,
        Diapered and diamond-dight,
    Flickered from the floor.

No mortal time I reckoned,
    Spirited away
For one ghostly second
    To where jewelled serpents play
        Like the fire-writing Hebraic,
        In mother-of-pearl mosaic
        Of flower-fields archaic—
    I let my fancy stray. . . .
        Till across these charmed errings
        Truth flashed:—it was the herrings
    I had brought from town late:
        The six silver herrings,
    On a Dutch-blue plate!

My dark humour shifted,
    Life in every pore,
Ecstatic and uplifted,
    I closed the larder door.

>   And there, phosphorescent
> As the herrings on the floor,
>   Gleamed the moon, evanescent,
>   Mother-of-pearl, iridescent.
>   Ah !—what made me quiescent
> To the glamoured path she shore !—
> While silver herrings flinging
>   Moonlight from a plate,
> Had set my soul singing
>   Like a bird to its mate !
>
> Rosamond Langbridge.

67. IN STILL MIDSUMMER NIGHT

In still midsummer night
    When the moon is late
And the stars all watery and white
    For her coming wait,

A spirit, whose eyes are possest
    By wonder new,
Passeth—her arms upon her breast
    Enrapt from the dew

In a raiment of azure fold
    With diaper
Of flower'd embroidery of gold
    Bestarr'd with silver.

The daisy folk are awake
    Their carpet to spread,
And the thron'd stars gazing on her make
    Fresh crowns for her head,

Netted in her floating hair
　As she drifteth free
Between the starriness of the air
　And the starry lea,

From the silent-shadow'd vale
　By the west wind drawn
Aloft to melt into the pale
　Moonrise of dawn.

Robert Bridges.

68. THE TRUANTS

Ere my heart beats too coldly and faintly
　To remember sad things, yet be gay,
I would sing a brief song of the world's little children
　Magic hath stolen away.

The primroses scattered by April,
　The stars of the wide Milky Way,
Cannot outnumber the hosts of the children
　Magic hath stolen away.

The buttercup green of the meadows,
　The snow of the blossoming may,
Lovelier are not than the legions of children
　Magic hath stolen away.

The waves tossing surf in the moonbeam,
　The albatross lone on the spray,
Alone know the tears wept in vain for the children
　Magic hath stolen away.

In vain : for at hush of the evening,
  When the stars twinkle into the grey,
Seems to echo the far-away calling of children
  Magic hath stolen away.
                              Walter de la Mare.

69. THE VOICE

The wind blows out of the gates of the day,
  The wind blows over the lonely of heart,
And the lonely of heart is withered away.
While the faeries dance in a place apart,
Shaking their milk-white feet in a ring,
Tossing their milk-white arms in the air ;
For they hear the wind laugh, and murmur and sing
Of a land where even the old are fair,
And even the wise are merry of tongue ;
But I heard a reed of Coolaney say,
" When the wind has laughed and murmured and sung
The lonely of heart is withered away ! "
                              William Butler Yeats.

70. FAERY SONG

Shed no tear ! oh shed no tear !
  The flower will bloom another year.
Weep no more ! oh weep no more !
Young buds sleep in the root's white core.
Dry your eyes ! oh dry your eyes !
For I was taught in Paradise
To ease my breast of melodies—
                    Shed no tear.

Overhead ! look overhead !
'Mong the blossoms white and red—
Look up, look up. I flutter now
On this flush pomegranate bough.
See me ! 'tis this silvery bill
Ever cures the good man's ill.
Shed no tear ! oh shed no tear !
The flower will bloom another year.
Adieu, adieu !—I fly, adieu !
I vanish in the heaven's blue—
     Adieu ! Adieu !

John Keats.

71. THE LITTLE WAVES OF BREFFNY

The grand road from the mountain goes shining to the sea,
 And there is traffic on it and many a horse and cart,
But the little roads of Cloonagh are dearer far to me,
 And the little roads of Cloonagh go rambling through my heart.

A great storm from the ocean goes shouting o'er the hill,
 And there is glory in it and terror on the wind,
But the haunted air of twilight is very strange and still,
 And the little winds of twilight are dearer to my mind.

The great waves of the Atlantic sweep storming on
    their way,
  Shining green and silver with the hidden herring
    shoal,
But the Little Waves of Breffny have drenched my
    heart in spray,
  And the Little Waves of Breffny go stumbling
    through my soul.

Eva Gore-Booth.

72. A BROKEN SONG

" *Where am I from?* " From the green hills of
        Erin.
" *Have I no song then?* " My songs are all sung.
" *What o' my love?* " 'Tis alone I am farin'.
Old grows my heart, an' my voice yet is young.

" *If she was tall?* " Like a king's own daughter.
" *If she was fair?* " Like a mornin' o' May.
When she'd come laughin' 'twas the running wather,
When she'd come blushin' 'twas the break o' day.

" *Where did she dwell?* " Where one'st I had my
    dwellin'.
" *Who loved her best?* " There's no one now will
    know.
" *Where is she gone?* " Och, why would I be tellin'!
Where she is gone there I can never go.

Moira O'Neill.

73. REQUIESCAT

Strew on her roses, roses,
    And never a spray of yew!
In quiet she reposes;
    Ah, would that I did too!

Her mirth the world required;
    She bathed it in smiles of glee.
But her heart was tired, tired,
    And now they let her be.

Her life was turning, turning,
    In mazes of heat and sound.
But for peace her soul was yearning,
    And now peace laps her round.

Her cabin'd, ample spirit,
    It flutter'd and fail'd for breath.
To-night it doth inherit
    The vasty hall of death.

                        Matthew Arnold.

74. THE GOING OF THE BATTERY
Wives' Lament (November 2, 1899)

O it was sad enough, weak enough, mad enough—
    Light in their loving as soldiers can be—
First to risk choosing them, leave alone losing them
Now, in far battle, beyond the South Sea!

—Rain came down drenchingly; but we unblenchingly
Trudged on beside them through mirk and through mire,
They stepping steadily—only too readily!—
Scarce as if stepping brought parting-time nigher.

Great guns were gleaming there, living things seeming there,
Cloaked in their tar-cloths, upmouthed to the night;
Wheels wet and yellow from axle to felloe,
Throats blank of sound, but prophetic to sight.

Gas-glimmers drearily, blearily, eerily
Lit our pale faces outstretched for one kiss,
While we stood prest to them, with a last quest to them
Not to court perils that honour could miss.

Sharp were those sighs of ours, blinded these eyes of ours,
When at last moved away under the arch
All we loved. Aid for them each woman prayed for them,
Treading back slowly the track of their march.

Someone said: "Nevermore will they come: evermore
Are they now lost to us." O it was wrong!
Though may be hard their ways, some Hand will guard their ways,
Bring them through safely, in brief time or long.

—Yet, voices haunting us, daunting us, taunting us,
Hint in the night-time when life beats are low
Other and graver things. . . . Hold we to braver
    things,
Wait we, in trust, what Time's fulness shall show.

Thomas Hardy.

75. THE SOLDIER

IF I should die, think only this of me:
    That there's some corner of a foreign field
That is for ever England. There shall be
    In that rich earth a richer dust concealed;
A dust whom England bore, shaped, made aware,
    Gave, once, her flowers to love, her ways to roam,
A body of England's, breathing English air,
    Washed by the rivers, blest by suns of home.

And think, this heart, all evil shed away,
    A pulse in the eternal mind, no less
        Gives somewhere back the thoughts by England
            given;
Her sights and sounds; dreams happy as her day;
    And laughter, learnt of friends; and gentleness,
        In hearts at peace, under an English heaven.

Rupert Brooke.

76. AND DID THOSE FEET

AND did those feet in ancient time
    Walk upon England's mountain green?
And was the holy Lamb of God
    On England's pleasant pastures seen?

And did the Countenance Divine
  Shine forth upon our clouded hills ?
And was Jerusalem builded here
  Among these dark Satanic mills ?

Bring me my bow of burning gold !
  Bring me my arrows of desire !
Bring me my spear : O clouds, unfold !
  Bring me my chariot of fire !

I will not cease from mental fight,
  Nor shall my sword sleep in my hand,
Till we have built Jerusalem
  In England's green and pleasant land.
William Blake.

77. INTO BATTLE

THE naked earth is warm with Spring,
  And with green grass and bursting trees
Leans to the sun's gaze glorying,
  And quivers in the sunny breeze ;

And Life is Colour and Warmth and Light,
  And a striving evermore for these ;
And he is dead who will not fight,
  And who dies fighting has increase.

The fighting man shall from the sun
  Take warmth, and life from the glowing earth ;
Speed with the light-foot winds to run,
  And with the trees to newer birth ;
And find, when fighting shall be done,
  Great rest, and fullness after dearth.

All the bright company of heaven
  Hold him in their high comradeship,
The Dog-Star, and the Sisters Seven,
  Orion's Belt and sworded hip.

The woodland trees that stand together,
  They stand to him each one a friend;
They gently speak in the windy weather;
  They guide to valley and ridges' end.

The kestrel hovering by day,
  And the little owls that call by night,
Bid him be swift and keen as they,
  As keen of ear, as swift of sight.

The blackbird sings to him, "Brother, brother,
  If this be the last song you shall sing
Sing well, for you may not sing another;
  Brother, sing."

In dreary, doubtful, waiting hours,
  Before the brazen frenzy starts,
The horses show him nobler powers;—
  O patient eyes, courageous hearts!

And when the burning moment breaks,
  And all things else are out of mind,
And only joy of battle takes
  Him by the throat, and makes him blind,

Through joy and blindness he shall know,
  Not caring much to know, that still
Nor lead nor steel shall reach him, so
  That it be not the Destined Will.

The thundering line of battle stands,
    And in the air Death moans and sings;
But Day shall clasp him with strong hands,
    And Night shall fold him in soft wings.

Julian Grenfell.

FLANDERS, *April* 1915.

78. THE DEAD

Blow out, you bugles, over the rich Dead!
    There's none of these so lonely and poor of old,
But, dying, has made us rarer gifts than gold.
These laid the world away; poured out the red
Sweet wine of youth; gave up the years to be
    Of work and joy, and that unhoped serene,
    That men call age; and those who would have been,
Their sons, they gave, their immortality.

Blow, bugles, blow! They brought us, for our dearth,
    Holiness, lacked so long, and Love, and Pain.
Honour has come back, as a king, to earth,
    And paid his subjects with a royal wage;
And Nobleness walks in our ways again,
    And we have come into our heritage.

Rupert Brooke.

79. A LEGEND OF YPRES

Before the throne the spirits of the slain
    With a loud voice importunately cried,
    "Oh, Lord of Hosts, whose name be glorified,
Scarce may the line one onslaught more sustain

Wanting our help.   Let it not be in vain,
  Not all in vain, Oh God, that we have died."
And smiling on them our good Lord replied,
" Begone then, foolish ones, and fight again."

Our eyes were holden, that we saw them not;
  Disheartened foes beheld—our prisoners said—
Behind us massed, a mighty host indeed,
Where no host was.   On comrades unforgot
  We thought, and knew that all those valiant dead
Forwent their rest to save us at our need.

Elinor Jenkins.

80. A GIRL'S SONG

THE Meuse and Marne have little waves;
  The slender poplars o'er them lean.
One day they will forget the graves
  That give the grass its living green.

Some brown French girl the rose will wear
  That springs above his comely head;
Will twine it in her russet hair,
  Nor wonder why it is so red.

His blood is in the rose's veins,
  His hair is in the yellow corn:
My grief is in the weeping rains
  And in the keening wind forlorn.

Flow softly, softly, Marne and Meuse;
  Tread lightly, all ye browsing sheep;
Fall tenderly, O silver dews,
  For here my dear Love lies asleep.

The earth is on his sealèd eyes,
    The beauty marred that was my pride;
Would I were lying where he lies,
    And sleeping sweetly by his side!

The Spring will come by Meuse and Marne,
    The birds be blithesome in the tree.
I heap the stones to make his cairn
    Where many sleep as sound as he.

                      Katharine Tynan.

81. SONG OF THE SOLDIERS' WIVES

At last! In sight of home again,
    Of home again;
No more to range and roam again
    As at that bygone time?
No more to go away from us
    And stay from us?—
Dawn, hold not long the day from us,
    But quicken it to prime!

Now all the town shall ring to them,
    Shall ring to them,
And we who love them cling to them
    And clasp them joyfully;
And cry, " O much we'll do for you
    Anew for you,
Dear Loves!—aye, draw and hew for you,
    Come back from oversea."

Some told us we should meet no more,
    Should meet no more;
Should wait, and wish, but greet no more
    Your faces round our fires;
That, in a while, uncharily
    And drearily
Men gave their lives—even wearily,
    Like those whom living tires.

And now you are nearing home again,
    Dears, home again;
No more, may be, to roam again
    As at that bygone time,
Which took you far away from us
    To stay from us;
Dawn, hold not long the day from us,
    But quicken it to prime!

Thomas Hardy.

82. PEACE

My soul, there is a country
    Far beyond the stars,
Where stands a wingèd sentry
    All skilful in the wars;
There, above noise and danger,
    Sweet Peace sits crowned with smiles,
And One born in a manger
    Commands the beauteous files.
He is thy gracious Friend,
    And, O my soul, awake!
Did in pure love descend
    To die here for thy sake;

If thou canst but get thither,
   There grows the flower of peace,
The rose that cannot wither,
   Thy fortress and thy ease.
Leave, then, thy foolish ranges,
   For none can thee secure,
But One, who never changes,
   Thy God, thy life, thy cure !

Henry Vaughan.

83. THE LAKE ISLE OF INNISFREE

I will arise and go now, and go to Innisfree,
   And a small cabin build there, of clay and wattles made ;
Nine bean rows will I have there, a hive for the honey-bee,
And live alone in the bee-loud glade.

And I shall have some peace there, for peace comes dropping slow,
Dropping from the veils of the morning to where the cricket sings,
There midnight's all a glimmer, and noon a purple glow,
And evening full of the linnet's wings.

I will arise and go now, for always night and day
I hear lake water lapping with low sounds by the shore;
While I stand on the roadway, or on the pavements gray,
I hear it in the deep heart's core.

William Butler Yeats.

84. MORNING THANKSGIVING

Thank God for sleep in the long quiet night,
    For the clear day calling through the little leaded panes,
For the shining well-water and the warm golden light,
    And the paths washed white by singing rains.

We thank Thee, O God, for exultation born
    Of the kiss of Thy winds, for life among the leaves,
For the whirring wings that pass about the wonder of the morn,
    For the changing plumes of swallows gliding upwards to their eaves.

For the treasure of the garden, the gillyflowers of gold,
    The prouder petalled tulips, the primrose full of spring,
For the crowded orchard boughs, and the swelling buds that hold
    A yet unwoven wonder, to Thee our praise we bring.

Thank God for good bread, for the honey in the comb,
    For the brown-shelled eggs, for the clustered blossoms set
Beyond the open window in a pink and cloudy foam,
    For the laughing loves among the branches set.

For the kind-faced women we bring our thanks to
    Thee,
  With shapely mothering arms and grave eyes
    clear and blithe,
For the tall young men, strong-thewed as men may be,
  For the old man bent above his scythe.

For earth's little secret and innumerable ways,
  For the carol and the colour, Lord, we bring
What things may be of thanks, and that Thou hast
    lent our days
  Eyes to see and ears to hear and lips to sing.
                              John Drinkwater.

85. A THANKSGIVING TO GOD FOR HIS HOUSE

Lord, Thou hast given me a cell
    Wherein to dwell;
A little house, whose humble roof
    Is weather-proof;
Under the spars of which I lie
    Both soft and dry;
Where Thou my chamber for to ward
    Hast set a guard
Of harmless thoughts, to watch and keep
    Me, while I sleep.
Low is my porch, as is my fate,
    Both void of state;
And yet the threshold of my door
    Is worn by th' poor,

Who thither come, and freely get
    Good words or meat;
Like as my parlour, so my hall
    And kitchen's small;
A little buttery, and therein
    A little bin
Which keeps my little loaf of bread
    Unclipt, unflay'd.
Some little sticks of thorn or briar
    Make me a fire,
Close by whose living coal I sit,
    And glow like it.
Lord, I confess, too, when I dine,
    The pulse is Thine,
And all those other bits, that be
    There placed by Thee;
The worts, the purslain, and the mess
    Of water-cress,
Which of Thy kindness Thou hast sent;
    And my content
Makes those, and my beloved beet
    To be more sweet.
'Tis Thou that crown'st my glittering heart
    With guiltless mirth;
And giv'st me wassail bowls to drink,
    Spiced to the brink.
Lord, 'tis Thy plenty-dropping hand,
    That soils my land;
And giv'st me for my bushel sown
    Twice ten for one.

Thou mak'st my teeming hen to lay
    Her egg each day;
Besides my healthful ewes to bear
    Me twins each year,
The while the conduits of my kine
    Run cream for wine.
All these, and better, Thou dost send
    Me, to this end,
That I should render, for my part,
    A thankful heart;
Which, fired with incense, I resign,
    As wholly Thine;
But the acceptance, that must be,
    My Christ, by Thee.

Robert Herrick.

86. VIRTUE

Sweet Day, so cool, so calm, so bright,
    The bridal of the earth and sky;
The dew shall weep thy fall to-night,
    For thou must die.

Sweet Rose, whose hue angry and brave
    Bids the rash gazer wipe his eye;
Thy root is ever in its grave,
    And thou must die.

Sweet Spring, full of sweet days and roses,
    A box where sweets compacted lie;
My music shows ye have your closes,
    And all must die.

Only a sweet and virtuous soul,
   Like seasoned timber, never gives;
But, though the whole world turn to coal,
   Then chiefly lives.

George Herbert.

DUCKS

I

From troubles of the world
   I turn to ducks,
Beautiful comical things
Sleeping or curled
Their heads beneath white wings
By water cool,
Or finding curious things
To eat in various mucks
Beneath the pool,
Tails uppermost, or waddling
Sailor-like on the shores
Of ponds, or paddling
—Left! right!—with fanlike feet
Which are for steady oars
When they (white galleys) float
Each bird a boat
Rippling at will the sweet
Wide waterway . . .
When night is fallen *you* creep
Upstairs, but drakes and dillies
Nest with pale water-stars,

Moonbeams and shadow bars,
And water-lilies:
Fearful too much to sleep
Since they've no locks
To click against the teeth
Of weasel and fox.
And warm beneath
Are eggs of cloudy green
Whence hungry rats and lean
Would stealthily suck
New life, but for the mien,
The bold ferocious mien
Of the mother-duck.

II

Yes, ducks are valiant things
On nests of twigs and straws,
And ducks are soothy things
And lovely on the lake
When that the sunlight draws
Thereon their pictures dim
In colours cool.
And when beneath the pool
They dabble, and when they swim
And make their rippling rings,
O ducks are beautiful things!

But ducks are comical things:—
As comical as you.
Quack!
They waddle round, they do.

They eat all sorts of things,
And then they quack.
By barn and stable and stack
They wander at their will,
But if you go too near
They look at you through black
Small topaz-tinted eyes
And wish you ill.
Triangular and clear
They leave their curious track
In mud at the water's edge,
And there amid the sedge
And slime they gobble and peer
Saying " Quack ! quack ! "

III

When God had finished the stars and whirl of coloured
    suns
He turned His mind from big things to fashion little
    ones,
Beautiful tiny things (like daisies) He made, and then
He made the comical ones in case the minds of men
    Should stiffen and become
    Dull, humourless and glum :
And so forgetful of their Maker be
As to take even themselves—*quite seriously.*
Caterpillars and cats are lively and excellent puns.
All God's jokes are good—even the practical ones !
And as for the duck, I think God must have smiled
    a bit

Seeing those bright eyes blink on the day He fashioned it.
And He's probably laughing still at the sound that came out of its bill!

Frederick William Harvey.

88. THE TIGER

Tiger, Tiger, burning bright
  In the forests of the night,
What immortal hand or eye
Could frame thy fearful symmetry?

In what distant deeps or skies
Burnt the fire of thine eyes?
On what wings dare he aspire?
What the hand dare seize the fire?

And what shoulder and what art
Could twist the sinews of thy heart?
And, when thy heart began to beat,
What dread hand? and what dread feet?

What the hammer? What the chain?
In what furnace was thy brain?
What the anvil? What dread grasp
Dare its deadly terrors clasp?

When the stars threw down their spears,
And water'd heaven with their tears,
Did He smile His work to see?
Did He who made the lamb make thee?

Tiger, Tiger, burning bright
In the forests of the night,
What immortal hand or eye
Dare frame thy fearful symmetry ?

William Blake.

89. THE SILKWORM

The beams of April, ere it goes,
   A worm, scarce visible, disclose;
All winter long content to dwell
The tenant of his native shell.
The same prolific season gives
The sustenance by which he lives,
The mulberry leaf, a simple store,
That serves him—till he needs no more!
For, his dimensions once complete,
Thenceforth none ever sees him eat;
Though, till his growing time be past,
Scarce ever is he seen to fast.

That hour arrived, his work begins;
He spins and weaves, and weaves and spins,
Till circle upon circle wound
Careless around him and around,
Conceals him with a veil, though slight,
Impervious to the keenest sight.
Thus self-enclosed, as in a cask,
At length he finishes his task:
And though a worm when he was lost,
Or caterpillar at the most,

When next we see him, wings he wears,
And in papilio-pomp appears;
Becomes oviparous; supplies
With future worms and future flies
The next-ensuing year;—and dies!

Well were it for the world, if all
Who creep about this earthly ball,
Though shorter-lived than most he be,
Were useful in their kind as he.

William Cowper.

90. THE NYMPH COMPLAINING FOR THE DEATH OF HER FAWN (*Extract*)

WITH sweetest milk and sugar first
    I it at my own fingers nursed;
And as it grew, so every day
It wax'd more white and sweet than they.
It had so sweet a breath! And oft
I blush'd to see its foot more soft
And white, shall I say than my hand?
Nay, any lady's of the land.

It is a wondrous thing how fleet
'Twas on those little silver feet;
With what a pretty skipping grace
It oft would challenge me the race;
And, when 't had left me far away,
'Twould stay, and run again, and stay;
For it was nimbler much than hinds,
And trod as if on the four winds.

I have a garden of my own,
But so with roses overgrown,
And lilies, that you would it guess
To be a little wilderness;
And all the spring-time of the year
It only lovèd to be there.
Among the beds of lilies I
Have sought it oft, where it should lie,
Yet could not, till itself would rise,
Find it, although before mine eyes;
For, in the flaxen lilies' shade,
It like a bank of lilies laid.
Upon the roses it would feed,
Until its lips e'en seem to bleed,
And then to me 'twould boldly trip,
And print those roses on my lip.
But all its chief delight was still
On roses thus itself to fill,
And its pure virgin limbs to fold
In whitest sheets of lilies cold:
Had it lived long, it would have been
Lilies without, roses within.

Andrew Marvell.

91. TO A CAT

CAT! who hast pass'd thy grand climacteric,
   How many mice and rats hast in thy days
Destroy'd?—How many tit bits stolen? Gaze
With those bright languid segments green, and prick

Those velvet ears—but pr'ythee do not stick
    Thy latent talons in me—and upraise
    Thy gentle mew—and tell me all thy frays
Of fish and mice, and rats and tender chick.
Nay, look not down, nor lick thy dainty wrists—
    For all the wheezy asthma—and for all
Thy tail's tip is nick'd off—and though the fists
    Of many a maid have given thee many a maul,
Still is that fur as soft as when the lists
    In youth thou enter'dst on glass-bottled wall.

John Keats.

92. SONNET

My mistress' eyes are nothing like the sun;
    Coral is far more red than her lips' red:
If snow be white, why then her breasts are dun;
If hairs be wires, black wires grow on her head.
I have seen roses damask'd, red and white,
But no such roses see I in her cheeks;
And in some perfumes is there more delight
Than in the breath that from my mistress reeks.
I love to hear her speak, yet well I know
That music hath a far more pleasing sound:
I grant I never saw a goddess go,
My mistress, when she walks, treads on the ground:
    And yet, by heaven, I think my love as rare
    As any she belied with false compare.

William Shakespeare.

93. SONNET

THE forward violet thus did I chide:
    Sweet thief, whence didst thou steal thy sweet
        that smells,
If not from my love's breath? The purple pride
Which on thy soft cheek for complexion dwells,
In my love's veins thou hast too grossly dyed.
The lily I condemnèd for thy hand,
And buds of marjoram had stol'n thy hair;
The roses fearfully on thorns did stand,
One blushing shame, another white despair;
A third, nor red nor white, had stol'n of both,
And to his robbery had annex'd thy breath;
But, for his theft, in pride of all his growth
A vengeful canker eat him up to death.
    More flowers I noted, yet I none could see
    But sweet or colour it had stol'n from thee.

William Shakespeare.

94. THE MILKMAID

ACROSS the grass I see her pass;
    She comes with tripping pace,—
A maid I know,—and March winds blow
    Her hair across her face;—
        With a hey, Dolly! ho, Dolly!
        Dolly shall be mine,
        Before the spray is white with May,
        Or blooms the eglantine.

The March winds blow. I watch her go;
  Her eye is brown and clear;
Her cheek is brown, and soft as down
  (To those who see it near!)—
    With a hey, Dolly! ho, Dolly!
      Dolly shall be mine,
        Before the spray is white with May,
          Or blooms the eglantine.

What has she not that those have got,—
  The dames that walk in silk!
If she undo her 'kerchief blue,
  Her neck is white as milk.
    With a hey, Dolly! ho, Dolly!
      Dolly shall be mine,
        Before the spray is white with May,
          Or blooms the eglantine.

Let those who will be proud and chill!
  For me, from June to June,
My Dolly's words are sweet as curds—
  Her laugh is like a tune;—
    With a hey, Dolly! ho, Dolly!
      Dolly shall be mine,
        Before the spray is white with May,
          Or blooms the eglantine.

Break, break to hear, O crocus-spear!
  O tall Lent-lilies, flame!
There'll be a bride at Easter-time,
  And Dolly is her name.

With a hey, Dolly! ho, Dolly!
    Dolly shall be mine,
Before the spray is white with May,
    Or blooms the eglantine.

Austin Dobson.

95. JOHNEEN

Sure he's five months old, an' he's two foot long,
    Baby Johneen;
Watch yerself now, for he's terrible sthrong,
    Baby Johneen.
An' his fists 'ill be up if ye make any slips,
He has finger-ends like the daisy-tips,
But he'll have ye attend to the words of his lips,
    Will Johneen.

There' nobody can rightly tell the colour of his eyes,
    This Johneen;
For they're partly o' the earth an' still they're partly
    o' the skies,
    Like Johneen.
So far as he's thravelled he's been laughin' all the way,
For the little soul is quare an' wise, the little heart is gay;
An' he likes the merry daffodils, he thinks they'd do to play
    With Johneen.

He'll sail a boat yet, if he only has his luck,
              Young Johneen,
For he takes to the wather like any little duck,
              Boy Johneen ;
Sure them are the hands now to pull on a rope,
An' nate feet for walkin' the deck on a slope,
But the ship she must wait a wee while yet, I hope,
              For Johneen.

For we couldn't do wantin' him, not just yet,
              Och, Johneen ;
'Tis you that are the daisy, an' you that are the pet,
              Wee Johneen.
Here's to your health, an' we'll dhrink it to-night.
Slainte gal, avic machree! live an' do right,
Slainte gal avourneen! may your days be bright,
              Johneen !
                      Moira O'Neill.

96. MY GARDEN

A GARDEN is a lovesome thing, God wot !
    Rose plot,
  Fringed pool,
Ferned grot—
    The veriest school
    Of peace ; and yet the fool
Contends that God is not—
Not God ! in gardens ! when the eve is cool ?
    Nay, but I have a sign ;
      'Tis very sure God walks in mine.
                      T. E. Brown.

97. THE GARDEN

How vainly men themselves amaze
  To win the palm, the oak, or bays;
And their incessant labours see
Crown'd from some single herb or tree,
Whose short and narrow-vergèd shade
Does prudently their toils upbraid;
While all the flowers and trees do close,
To weave the garlands of repose!

Fair Quiet, have I found thee here,
And Innocence, thy sister dear?
Mistaken long, I sought you then
In busy companies of men.
Your sacred plants, if here below,
Only among the plants will grow:
Society is all but rude
To this delicious solitude.

No white nor red was ever seen
So amorous as this lovely green.
Fond lovers, cruel as their flame,
Cut in these trees their mistress' name:
Little, alas! they know or heed
How far these beauties hers exceed!
Fair trees! wheresoe'er your barks I wound,
No name shall but your own be found.

When we have run our passions' heat,
Love hither makes his best retreat.
The gods, who mortal beauty chase,
Still in a tree did end their race;
Apollo hunted Daphne so,
Only that she might laurel grow;
And Pan did after Syrinx speed
Not as a nymph, but for a reed.

What wondrous life is this I lead!
Ripe apples drop about my head;
The luscious clusters of the vine
Upon my mouth do crush their wine;
The nectarine and curious peach
Into my hands themselves do reach;
Stumbling on melons, as I pass,
Ensnared with flowers, I fall on grass.

Meanwhile the mind, from pleasure less,
Withdraws into its happiness;
The mind, that ocean where each kind
Does straight its own resemblance find;
Yet it creates, transcending these,
Far other worlds, and other seas;
Annihilating all that's made
To a green thought in a green shade.

Here at the fountain's sliding foot,
Or at some fruit-tree's mossy root,
Casting the body's vest aside,
My soul into the boughs does glide;

There, like a bird, it sits and sings,
Then whets and combs its silver wings,
And, till prepared for longer flight,
Waves in its plumes the various light.

Such was that happy garden-state
While man there walk'd without a mate:
After a place so pure and sweet,
What other help could yet be meet!
But 'twas beyond a mortal's share
To wander solitary there:
Two Paradises 'twere in one
To live in Paradise alone.

How well the skilful gardener drew
Of flowers and herbs this dial new;
Where, from above, the milder sun
Does through a fragrant zodiac run:
And, as it works, the industrious bee
Computes its time as well as we!
How could such sweet and wholesome hours
Be reckon'd but with herbs and flowers?

Andrew Marvell.

98. THE QUESTION

I DREAMED that, as I wandered by the way,
   Bare winter suddenly was changed to spring,
And gentle odours led my steps astray,
   Mixed with a sound of waters murmuring

Along a shelving bank of turf, which lay
   Under a copse, and hardly dared to fling
Its green arms round the bosom of the stream,
But kissed it and then fled, as thou mightest in dream.

There grew pied wind-flowers and violets,
   Daisies, those pearled Arcturi of the earth,
The constellated flower that never sets;
   Faint oxlips; tender bluebells, at whose birth
The sod scarce heaved; and that tall flower that
     wets—
   Like a child, half in tenderness and mirth—
Its mother's face with heaven-collected tears,
When the low wind, its playmate's voice, it hears.

And in the warm hedge grew lush eglantine,
   Green cowbind and the moonlight-coloured May,
And cherry-blossoms, and white cups, whose wine
   Was the bright dew, yet drained not by the day;
And wild roses, and ivy serpentine,
   With its dark buds and leaves, wandering astray;
And flowers azure, black, and streaked with gold,
Fairer than any wakened eyes behold.

And nearer to the river's trembling edge
   There grew broad flag-flowers, purple prankt with
     white,
And starry river buds among the sedge,
   And floating water-lilies, broad and bright,

Which lit the oak that overhung the hedge
  With moonlight beams of their own watery light;
And bulrushes, and reeds of such deep green
As soothed the dazzled eye with sober sheen.

Methought that of these visionary flowers
  I made a nosegay, bound in such a way
That the same hues, which in their natural bowers
  Were mingled or opposed, the like array
Kept these imprisoned children of the Hours
  Within my hand,—and then, elate and gay,
I hastened to the spot whence I had come,
That I might there present it!—oh! to whom?

Percy Bysshe Shelley.

99. THE PINES

Above the pine the ghostly moonlight lingers
    Or plays along the fir,
The elves are tracing with their slender fingers
    Their paths of gossamer,
The trees are crooning softly, saintly, lowly,
    Like whispering acolytes,
The heart-song of the forest deep and holy
    As northern lights.

From hoary oak and alder hang the mosses,
    Time's ancient tapestrie;
The molten moon-fire crosses and recrosses
    In silvery filigree,

The stars peep from the hyaline, enchanted
    Deep waters of the stream,
And every break and brake and bank is haunted
    By visions as a dream.

Low in the darkling fretwork, arborescent,
    The trailing swamp mists rise
Impalpable as frostwork's evanescent
    Shimmering subtleties.
Afar, the antlered moose is calling plaintly
    Through covert drear and dim,
And from the thicket hedge enticing faintly,
    The female answers him.
Across the north the fair aurora glistening
    Leans on the heavenly signs,
Night !—and yearning as a child I'm listening
    The heart-song of the pines.

Patrick MacGill.

100. THE ROADSIDE PINES

WE paused beneath the shadow of the pines.
    'Twas very still, no breeze their branches stirred.
Only the sweet, rare twittering of a bird
Spoke, faintly heard.

Silent they stood—most grave and calm;
Hearkening the benediction strong
Of unseen angels, and the triumph song
Roll heaven along.

High priests we deemed them, serving at a shrine.
They drew a blessing down as they adored.
Their secret balm of peace was softly poured
On hearts restored.

Ethel L. Fowler.

101. THE GUARDIAN-ANGEL (*Extract*)

A Picture at Fano

I

Dear and great Angel, wouldst thou only leave
    That child, when thou hast done with him, for me !
Let me sit all the day here, that when eve
    Shall find performed thy special ministry,
And time come for departure, thou, suspending
Thy flight, mayst see another child for tending,
    Another still, to quiet and retrieve.

II

Then I shall feel thee step one step, no more,
    From where thou standest now, to where I gaze,
—And suddenly my head is covered o'er
    With those wings, white above the child who prays
Now on that tomb--and I shall feel thee guarding
Me, out of all the world ; for me, discarding
    Yon heaven thy home, that waits and opes its door.

III

I would not look up thither past thy head
   Because the door opes, like that child, I know,
For I should have thy gracious face instead,
   Thou bird of God! And wilt thou bend me low
Like him, and lay, like his, my hands together,
And lift them up to pray, and gently tether
   Me, as thy lamb there, with thy garment's spread?

IV

If this was ever granted, I would rest
   My head beneath thine, while thy healing hands
Close-covered both my eyes beside thy breast,
   Pressing the brain, which too much thought expands,
Back to its proper size again, and smoothing
Distortion down till every nerve had soothing,
   And all lay quiet, happy and suppressed.

V

How soon all worldly wrong would be repaired!
   I think how I should view the earth and skies
And sea, when once again my brow was bared
   After thy healing, with such different eyes.
O world, as God has made it! All is beauty:
And knowing this, is love, and love is duty.
   What further may be sought for or declared?

    .   .   .   .   .

Robert Browning.

102. SHERWOOD

Sherwood in the twilight, is Robin Hood awake?
  Grey and ghostly shadows are gliding through the brake,
Shadows of the dappled deer, dreaming of the morn,
Dreaming of a shadowy man that winds a shadowy horn.

Robin Hood is here again : all his merry thieves
Hear a ghostly bugle-note shivering through the leaves,
Calling as he used to call, faint and far away,
In Sherwood, in Sherwood, about the break of day.

Merry, merry England has kissed the lips of June :
All the wings of fairyland were here beneath the moon,
Like a flight of rose-leaves fluttering in a mist
Of opal and ruby and pearl and amethyst.

Merry, merry England is waking as of old,
With eyes of blither hazel and hair of brighter gold :
For Robin Hood is here again beneath the bursting spray
In Sherwood, in Sherwood, about the break of day.

Love is in the greenwood building him a house
Of wild rose and hawthorn and honeysuckle boughs :
Love is in the greenwood, dawn is in the skies,
And Marian is waiting with a glory in her eyes.

Hark ! the dazzled laverock climbs the golden steep !
Marian is waiting : is Robin Hood asleep ?
Round the fairy grass-rings frolic elf and fay,
In Sherwood, in Sherwood, about the break of day.

Oberon, Oberon, rake away the gold,
Rake away the red leaves, roll away the mould,
Rake away the gold leaves, roll away the red,
And wake Will Scarlett from his leafy forest bed.

Friar Tuck and Little John are riding down together,
With quarter-staff and drinking-can and grey goose feather.
The dead are coming back again, the years are rolled away
In Sherwood, in Sherwood, about the break of day.

Softly over Sherwood the south wind blows.
All the heart of England hid in every rose
Hears across the greenwood the sunny whisper leap,
Sherwood in the red dawn, is Robin Hood asleep ?

Hark, the voice of England wakes him as of old
And, shattering the silence with a cry of brighter gold,
Bugles in the greenwood echo from the steep,
Sherwood in the red dawn, is Robin Hood asleep ?

Where the deer are gliding down the shadowy glen
All across the glades of fern he calls his merry men—
Doublets of the Lincoln green glancing through the May
In Sherwood, in Sherwood, about the break of day—

Calls them and they answer—from aisles of oak and ash
Rings the *Follow! Follow!* and the boughs begin to crash,
The ferns begin to flutter, and the flowers begin to fly,
And through the crimson dawning the robber band goes by.

Robin! Robin! Robin! All his merry thieves
Answer as the bugle-note shivers through the leaves,
Calling as he used to call, faint and far away,
In Sherwood, in Sherwood, about the break of day.

Alfred Noyes.

103. THE LADY OF SHALOTT

PART I

O<small>N</small> either side the river lie
    Long fields of barley and of rye,
That clothe the wold and meet the sky;
And thro' the field the road runs by
    To many-tower'd Camelot;
And up and down the people go,
Gazing where the lilies blow
Round an island there below,
    The island of Shalott.

Willows whiten, aspens quiver,
Little breezes dusk and shiver
Thro' the wave that runs for ever
By the island in the river
    Flowing down to Camelot.
Four gray walls, and four gray towers,
Overlook a space of flowers,
And the silent isle imbowers
    The Lady of Shalott.

By the margin, willow-veil'd,
Slide the heavy barges, trail'd
By slow horses; and unhail'd
The shallop flitteth silken-sail'd
    Skimming down to Camelot:
But who hath seen her wave her hand?
Or at the casement seen her stand?
Or is she known in all the land,
    The Lady of Shalott?

Only reapers, reaping early
In among the bearded barley,
Hear a song that echoes cheerly
From the river winding clearly,
    Down to tower'd Camelot:
And by the moon the reaper weary,
Piling sheaves in uplands airy,
Listening, whispers, " 'Tis the fairy
    Lady of Shalott."

PART II

There she weaves by night and day
A magic web with colours gay.
She has heard a whisper say,
A curse is on her if she stay
    To look down to Camelot.
She knows not what the curse may be,
And so she weaveth steadily,
And little other care hath she,
    The Lady of Shalott.

And moving thro' a mirror clear
That hangs before her all the year,
Shadows of the world appear.
There she sees the highway near
    Winding down to Camelot :
There the river eddy whirls,
And there the surly village-churls,
And the red cloaks of market girls,
    Pass onward from Shalott.

Sometimes a troop of damsels glad,
An abbot on an ambling pad,
Sometimes a curly shepherd-lad,
Or long-hair'd page in crimson clad,
    Goes by to tower'd Camelot ;
And sometimes thro' the mirror blue
The knights come riding two and two :
She hath no loyal knight and true,
    The Lady of Shalott.

But in her web she still delights
To weave the mirror's magic sights,
For often thro' the silent nights
A funeral, with plumes and lights
      And music, went to Camelot :
Or when the moon was overhead,
Came two young lovers lately wed ;
" I am half sick of shadows," said
      The Lady of Shalott.

PART III

A bow-shot from her bower-eaves,
He rode between the barley-sheaves,
The sun came dazzling thro' the leaves,
And flamed upon the brazen greaves
      Of bold Sir Lancelot.
A red-cross knight for ever kneel'd
To a lady in his shield,
That sparkled on the yellow field,
      Beside remote Shalott.

The gemmy bridle glitter'd free,
Like to some branch of stars we see
Hung in the golden Galaxy.
The bridle bells rang merrily
      As he rode down to Camelot,
And from his blazon'd baldric slung
A mighty silver bugle hung,
And as he rode his armour rung,
      Beside remote Shalott.

All in the blue unclouded weather
Thick-jewell'd shone the saddle-leather,
The helmet and the helmet-feather
Burn'd like one burning flame together,
    As he rode down to Camelot.
As often thro' the purple night,
Below the starry clusters bright,
Some bearded meteor, trailing light,
    Moves over still Shalott.

His broad clear brow in sunlight glow'd;
On burnish'd hooves his war-horse trode;
From underneath his helmet flow'd
His coal-black curls as on he rode,
    As he rode down to Camelot.
From the bank and from the river
He flash'd into the crystal mirror,
"Tirra lirra," by the river
    Sang Sir Lancelot.

She left the web, she left the loom,
She made three paces thro' the room,
She saw the water-lily bloom,
She saw the helmet and the plume,
    She look'd down to Camelot.
Out flew the web and floated wide;
The mirror crack'd from side to side;
"The curse is come upon me," cried
    The Lady of Shalott.

PART IV

In the stormy east-wind straining,
The pale yellow woods were waning,
The broad stream in his banks complaining,
Heavily the low sky raining
      Over tower'd Camelot;
Down she came and found a boat
Beneath a willow left afloat,
And round about the prow she wrote
      The Lady of Shalott.

And down the river's dim expanse—
Like some bold seër in a trance,
Seeing all his own mischance—
With a glassy countenance
      Did she look to Camelot.
And at the closing of the day
She loosed the chain, and down she lay;
The broad stream bore her far away,
      The Lady of Shalott.

Lying, robed in snowy white
That loosely flew to left and right—
The leaves upon her falling light—
Thro' the noises of the night,
      She floated down to Camelot.
And as the boat-head wound along
The willowy hills and fields among,
They heard her singing her last song,
      The Lady of Shalott.

Heard a carol, mournful, holy,
Chanted loudly, chanted lowly,
Till her blood was frozen slowly,
And her eyes were darken'd wholly,
    Turn'd to tower'd Camelot;
For ere she reach'd upon the tide
The first house by the water-side,
Singing in her song she died,
    The Lady of Shalott.

Under tower and balcony,
By garden-wall and gallery,
A gleaming shape she floated by,
Dead-pale between the houses high,
    Silent into Camelot.
Out upon the wharfs they came,
Knight and burgher, lord and dame,
And round the prow they read her name,
    The Lady of Shalott.

Who is this? and what is here?
And in the lighted palace near
Died the sound of royal cheer;
And they cross'd themselves for fear,
    All the knights at Camelot:
But Lancelot mused a little space;
He said, " She has a lovely face;
God in His mercy lend her grace,
    The Lady of Shalott."

                Alfred Tennyson.

104. THE SOULS OF THE SLAIN

I

The thick lids of night closed upon me
  Alone at the Bill
  Of the Isle by the Race*—
Many-caverned, bald, wrinkled of face—
And with darkness and silence the spirit was on me
  To brood and be still.

II

No wind fanned the flats of the ocean,
  Or promontory sides,
  Or the ooze by the strand,
  Or the bent-bearded slope of the land,
Whose base took its rest amid everlong motion
  Of criss-crossing tides.

III

Soon from out of the Southward seemed nearing
  A whirr, as of wings
  Waved by mighty-vanned flies,
  Or by night-moths of measureless size,
And in softness and smoothness well-nigh beyond hearing
  Of corporal things.

* The " Race " is the turbulent sea-area off the Bill of Portland, where contrary tides meet.

IV

And they bore to the bluff, and alighted—
          A dim-discerned train
          Of sprites without mould,
    Frameless souls none might touch or might hold—
On the ledge by the turreted lantern, far-sighted
          By men of the main.

V

And I heard them say " Home ! " and I knew them
          For souls of the felled
          On the earth's nether bord
    Under Capricorn, whither they'd warred,
And I neared in my awe, and gave heedfulness to them
          With breathings inheld.

VI

Then, it seemed, there approached from the northward
          A senior soul-flame
          Of the like filmy hue :
    And he met them and spake : " Is it you,
O my men ? " Said they, " Aye ! We bear homeward and hearthward
          To list to our fame ! "

VII

" I've flown there before you," he said then :
        " Your households are well ;
        But—your kin linger less
    On your glory and war-mightiness
Than on dearer things."—" Dearer ? " cried these from the dead then,
        " Of what do they tell ? "

VIII

" Some mothers muse sadly, and murmur
        Your doings as boys—
        Recall the quaint ways
    Of your babyhood's innocent days.
Some pray that, ere dying, your faith had grown firmer,
        And higher your joys.

IX

" A father broods : ' Would I had set him
        To some humble trade,
        And so slacked his high fire,
    And his passionate martial desire ;
Had told him no stories to woo him and whet him
        To this dire crusade ! ' "

X

" And, General, how hold out our sweethearts,
        Sworn loyal as doves ? "
        — " Many mourn ; many think

It is not unattractive to prink
Them in sables for heroes. Some fickle and fleet hearts
    Have found them new loves."

XI

" And our wives ? " quoth another resignedly,
    " Dwell they on our deeds ? "
    —" Deeds of home ; that live yet
Fresh as new—deeds of fondness or fret ;
Ancient words that were kindly expressed or unkindly,
    These, these have their heeds."

XII

—" Alas! then it seems that our glory
    Weighs less in their thought
    Than our old homely acts,
And the long-ago commonplace facts
Of our lives—held by us as scarce part of our story,
    And rated as nought ! "

XIII

Then bitterly some : " Was it wise now
    To raise the tomb-door
    For such knowledge ? Away ! "
But the rest : " Fame we prized till to-day ;
Yet that hearts keep us green for old kindness we prize now
    A thousand times more ! "

XIV

Thus speaking, the trooped apparitions
        Began to disband
        And resolve them in two :
Those whose record was lovely and true
Bore to northward for home : those of bitter traditions
        Again left the land,

XV

And, towering to seaward in legions,
        They paused at a spot
        Overbending the Race—
That engulphing, ghast, sinister place—
Whither headlong they plunged, to the fathomless regions
        Of myriads forgot.

XVI

And the spirits of those who were homing
        Passed on, rushingly,
        Like the Pentecost Wind;
And the whirr of their wayfaring thinned
And surceased on the sky, and but left in the gloaming
        Sea-mutterings and me.

                      Thomas Hardy.

December 1899.

105. BY THE STATUE OF KING CHARLES AT CHARING CROSS

Sombre and rich, the skies;
  Great glooms, and starry plains.
Gently the night wind sighs;
Else a vast silence reigns.

The splendid silence clings
Around me: and around
The saddest of all kings
Crowned, and again discrowned.

Comely and calm, he rides
Hard by his own Whitehall:
Only the night wind glides:
No crowds, nor rebels, brawl.

Gone, too, his Court; and yet,
The stars his courtiers are:
Stars in their stations set;
And every wandering star.

Alone he rides, alone,
The fair and fatal king:
Dark night is all his own,
That strange and solemn thing.

Which are more full of fate:
The stars; or those sad eyes?
Which are more still and great:
Those brows; or the dark skies?

Although his whole heart yearn
In passionate tragedy:
Never was face so stern
With sweet austerity.

Vanquished in life, his death
By beauty made amends:
The passing of his breath
Won his defeated ends.

Brief life and hapless? Nay:
Through death, life grew sublime.
Speak after sentence? Yea:
And to the end of time.

Armoured he rides, his head
Bare to the stars of doom:
He triumphs now, the dead,
Beholding London's gloom.

Our weaker spirit faints,
Vexed in the world's employ:
His soul was of the saints;
And art to him was joy.

King, tried in fires of woe!
Men hunger for thy grace:
And through the night I go,
Loving thy mournful face.

Yet, when the city sleeps;
When all the cries are still:
The stars and heavenly deeps
Work out a perfect will.

Lionel Johnson.

106. IN LADY STREET

All day long the traffic goes
In Lady Street by dingy rows
Of sloven houses, tattered shops—
Fried fish, old clothes and fortune-tellers—
Tall trams on silver-shining rails,
With grinding wheels and swaying tops,
And lorries with their corded bales,
And screeching cars. " Buy, buy !" the sellers
Of rags and bones and sickening meat
Cry all day long in Lady Street.

And when the sunshine has its way
In Lady Street, then all the grey
Dull desolation grows in state
More dull and grey and desolate,
And the sun is a shamefast thing,
A lord not comely-housed, a god
Seeing what gods must blush to see,
A song where it is ill to sing,
And each gold ray despiteously
Lies like a gold ironic rod.

Yet one grey man in Lady Street
Looks for the sun. He never bent
Life to his will, his travelling feet
Have scaled no cloudy continent,
Nor has the sickle-hand been strong.
He lives in Lady Street; a bed,
Four cobwebbed walls.

                        But all day long
A time is singing in his head
Of youth in Gloucester lanes. He hears
The wind among the barley-blades,
The tapping of the woodpeckers
On the smooth beeches, thistle-spades
Slicing the sinewy roots; he sees
The hooded filberts in the copse
Beyond the loaded orchard trees,
The netted avenues of hops;
He smells the honeysuckle thrown
Along the hedge. He lives alone,
Alone—yet not alone, for sweet
Are Gloucester lanes in Lady Street.

Aye, Gloucester lanes. For down below
The cobwebbed room this grey man plies
A trade, a coloured trade. A show
Of many-coloured merchandise
Is in his shop. Brown filberts there,
And apples red with Gloucester air,
And cauliflowers he keeps, and round
Smooth marrows grown on Gloucester ground,

Fat cabbages and yellow plums,
And gaudy brave chrysanthemums.
And times a glossy pheasant lies
Among his store, not Tyrian dyes
More rich than are the neck-feathers;
And times a prize of violets,
Or dewy mushrooms satin-skinned,
And times an unfamiliar wind
Robbed of its woodland favour stirs
Gay daffodils this grey man sets
Among his treasure.

                        All day long
In Lady Street the traffic goes
By dingy houses, desolate rows
Of shops that stare like hopeless eyes.
Day long the sellers cry their cries,
The fortune-tellers tell no wrong
Of lives that know not any right,
And drift, that has not even the will
To drift, toils through the day until
The wage of sleep is won at night.
But this grey man heeds not at all
The hell of Lady Street. His stall
Of many-coloured merchandise
He makes a shining paradise,
As all day long chrysanthemums
He sells, and red and yellow plums
And cauliflowers. In that one spot
Of Lady Street the sun is not

Ashamed to shine and send a rare
Shower of colour through the air;
The grey man says the sun is sweet
On Gloucester lanes in Lady Street.

John Drinkwater.

107. TITHONUS

The woods decay, the woods decay and fall,
　　The vapours weep their burthen to the ground,
Man comes and tills the field and lies beneath,
And after many a summer dies the swan.
Me only cruel immortality
Consumes: I wither slowly in thine arms,
Here at the quiet limit of the world,
A white-hair'd shadow roaming like a dream
The ever silent spaces of the East,
Far-folded mists, and gleaming halls of morn.

　Alas! for this gray shadow, once a man—
So glorious in his beauty and thy choice,
Who madest him thy chosen, that he seem'd
To his great heart none other than a God!
I ask'd thee, "Give me immortality!"
Then didst thou grant mine asking with a smile,
Like wealthy men who care not how they give.
But thy strong Hours indignant work'd their wills,
And beat me down and marred and wasted me,
And tho' they could not end me, left me maim'd
To dwell in presence of immortal youth,

Immortal age beside immortal youth,
And all I was, in ashes. Can thy love,
Thy beauty, make amends, tho' even now,
Close over us, the silver star, thy guide,
Shines in those tremulous eyes that fill with tears
To hear me ? Let me go : take back thy gift :
Why should a man desire in any way
To vary from the kindly race of men,
Or pass beyond the goal of ordinance
Where all should pause, as is most meet for all?

  A soft air fans the cloud apart ; there comes
A glimpse of that dark world where I was born.
Once more the old mysterious glimmer steals
From thy pure brows, and from thy shoulders pure,
And bosom beating with a heart renew'd.
Thy cheek begins to redden thro' the gloom,
Thy sweet eyes brighten slowly close to mine,
Ere yet they blind the stars, and the wild team
Which love thee, yearning for thy yoke, arise,
And shake the darkness from their loosen'd manes,
And beat the twilight into flakes of fire.

  Lo ! ever thus thou growest beautiful
In silence, then before thine answer given
Departest, and thy tears are on my cheek.

  Why wilt thou ever scare me with thy tears,
And make me tremble lest a saying learnt,
In days far-off, on that dark earth, be true ?
" The Gods themselves cannot recall their gifts."

Ay me! ay me! with what another heart
In days far-off, and with what other eyes
I used to watch—if I be he that watch'd—
The lucid outline forming round thee; saw
The dim curls kindle into sunny rings;
Changed with thy mystic change, and felt my blood
Glow with the glow that slowly crimson'd all
Thy presence and thy portals, while I lay,
Mouth, forehead, eyelids, growing dewy-warm
With kisses balmier than half-opening buds
Of April, and could hear the lips that kiss'd
Whispering I knew not what of wild and sweet,
Like that strange song I heard Apollo sing,
While Ilion like a mist rose into towers.

Yet hold me not for ever in thine East:
How can my nature longer mix with thine?
Coldly thy rosy shadows bathe me, cold
Are all thy lights, and cold my wrinkled feet
Upon thy glimmering thresholds, when the steam
Floats up from those dim fields about the homes
Of happy men that have the power to die,
And grassy barrows of the happier dead.
Release me, and restore me to the ground;
Thou seëst all things, thou wilt see my grave:
Thou wilt renew thy beauty morn by morn;
I earth in earth forget these empty courts,
And thee returning on thy silver wheels.

Alfred Tennyson.

108. TO THE POETS

Bards of Passion and of Mirth,
  Ye have left your souls on earth !
Have ye souls in heaven too,
Double-liv'd in regions new ?
Yes, and those of heaven commune
With the spheres of sun and moon;
With the noise of fountains wondrous,
And the parle of voices thund'rous;
With the whisper of heaven's trees
And one another, in soft ease
Seated on Elysian lawns
Brows'd by none but Dian's fawns;
Underneath large blue-bells tented,
Where the daisies are rose-scented,
And the rose herself has got
Perfume which on earth is not;
Where the nightingale doth sing
Not a senseless, trancèd thing,
But divine melodious truth,
Philosophic numbers smooth,
Tales and golden histories
Of heaven and its mysteries.

  Thus ye live on high, and then
On the earth ye live again;
And the souls ye left behind you
Teach us, here, the way to find you,
Where your other souls are joying
Never slumber'd, never cloying.

Here, your earth-born souls still speak
To mortals, of their little week;
Of their sorrows and delights;
Of their passions and their spites;
Of their glory and their shame;
What does strengthen and what maim.
Thus ye teach us, every day,
Wisdom, though fled far away.

Bards of Passion and of Mirth,
Ye have left your souls on earth!
Ye have souls in heaven too,
Double-liv'd in regions new!

John Keats.

THE END

INDEX OF FIRST LINES

	PAGE
A flock of sheep that leisurely pass by (*W. Wordsworth*)	95
A garden is a lovesome thing, God wot! (*T. E. Brown*)	127
A pure white mantle blotted out (*A. Noyes*)	13
Above the pine the ghostly moonlight lingers (*P. MacGill*)	132
Abroad on a winter's night there ran (*F. Sidgwick*)	88
Across the grass I see her pass (*A. Dobson*)	124
Ah, broken is the golden bowl! (*E. A. Poe*)	62
All day long the traffic goes (*J. Drinkwater*)	152
All suddenly the wind comes soft (*R. Brooke*)	81
And did those feet in ancient time (*W. Blake*)	104
At last! in sight of home again (*T. Hardy*)	109
Austere and clad in sombre robes of grey (*J. Drinkwater*)	81
Bards of Passion and of Mirth (*J. Keats*)	158
Before the throne the spirits of the slain (*E. Jenkins*)	107
Blow out, you bugles, over the rich Dead (*R. Brooke*)	107
Blow trumpet, for the world is white with May (*A. Tennyson*)	15
Bold Robin has robed him in ghostly attire (*T. L. Peacock*)	20
By the short cut to Rosses a fairy girl I met (*N. Chesson*)	30
Cat! who has pass'd thy grand climacteric (*J. Keats*)	122
Come, sweetheart, listen, for I have a thing (*J. Drinkwater*)	2
Come, tumble up, Lord Nelson (*D. Clark*)	18
Day! (*R. Browning*)	92
Dear and great Angel, wouldst thou only leave (*R. Browning*)	134
Elsie was a maiden fair (*F Thompson*)	40
Ere my heart beats too coldly and faintly (*W. de la Mare*)	98
Faster than fairies, faster than witches (*R. L. Stevenson*)	24
From troubles of the world (*F. W. Harvey*)	116
Gaily bedight (*E. A. Poe*)	47
Go down to Kew in lilac-time (*A. Noyes*)	5
Golden-winged, silver-winged (*C. G. Rossetti*)	38
How vainly men themselves amaze (*A. Marvell*)	128
I dreamed that, as I wandered by the way (*P. B. Shelley*)	130
I fear that Puck is dead—it is so long (*E. Lee-Hamilton*)	29
I saw the moon so broad and bright (*J. Stephens*)	94

INDEX OF FIRST LINES

	PAGE
I went into the larder (*R. Langbridge*)	95
I will arise and go now, and go to Innisfree (*W. B. Yeats*)	111
I wish I were where Helen lies (*Old Ballad*)	59
If I should die, think only this of me (*R. Brooke*)	104
If I were Lord of Tartary (*W. de la Mare*)	25
In numbers, and but these few (*R. Herrick*)	91
In still midsummer night (*R. Bridges*)	97
In summer, on the headlands (*M. Arnold*)	44
In the golden glade the chestnuts are fallen all (*R. Bridges*)	85
In the greenest of our valleys (*E. A. Poe*)	52
It was many and many a year ago (*E. A. Poe*)	53
Lord, Thou hast given me a cell (*R. Herrick*)	113
Morning, evening, noon and night (*R. Browning*)	67
My mistress' eyes are nothing like the sun (*W. Shakespeare*)	123
My soul, there is a country (*H. Vaughan*)	110
Nymph, nymph, what are your beads ? (*H. Monro*)	27
O holy virgin, clad in purest white (*W. Blake*)	92
O it was sad enough, weak enough, mad enough (*T. Hardy*)	102
O thou with dewy locks, who lookest down (*W. Blake*)	82
O what can ail thee, knight-at-arms (*J. Keats*)	50
O where have ye been, Lord Randal, my son (*Old Ballad*)	60
On either side the river lie (*A. Tennyson*)	138
On Newlyn Hill the gorse is bright (*C. Garstin*)	83
Open your doors and let me in (*Christmas Play*)	76
Outlanders, whence come ye last ? (*W. Morris*)	86
Over the frozen plains snow-white (*R. L. Gales*)	14
Saint George he was a fighting man (*from " Punch "*)	16
See, whirling snow sprinkles the starvèd fields (*R. Bridges*)	3
Seek up and down, both fair and brown (*W. Allingham*)	35
She stepped upon Sicilian grass (*J. Ingelow*)	64
She was a lady great and splendid (*W. Watson*)	48
Shed no tear ! oh, shed no tear ! (*J. Keats*)	99
Sherwood in the twilight, is Robin Hood awake ? (*A. Noyes*)	136
Sombre and rich the skies (*L. Johnson*)	150
Spring, the Travelling Man, has been here (*W. M. Letts*)	4
Sure he's five months old, an' he's two foot long (*M. O'Neill*)	126
Sure maybe ye've heard the storm-thrush (*M. O'Neill*)	37
Strew on her roses, roses (*M. Arnold*)	102
Sweet day, so cool, so calm, so bright (*G. Herbert*)	115
Swiftly walk over the western wave (*P. B. Shelley*)	93

INDEX OF FIRST LINES

	PAGE
Tell the tune his feet beat (*A. S. Cripps*)	20
Thank God for sleep in the long quiet night (*J. Drinkwater*)	112
The beams of April, ere it goes (*W. Cowper*)	120
The forward violet thus did I chide (*W. Shakespeare*)	124
The grand road from the mountain goes shining to the sea (*E. Gore-Booth*)	100
The Meuse and Marne have little waves (*K. Tynan*)	108
The mountain sheep are sweeter (*T. L. Peacock*)	22
The naked earth is warm with spring (*J. Grenfell*)	105
The pinks along my garden walks (*R. Bridges*)	84
The raining hour is done (*J. Drinkwater*)	83
The storm-cock in the apple-trees (*W. M. E. F.*)	3
The thick lids of night closed upon me (*T. Hardy*)	145
The warm sun is failing, the bleak wind is wailing (*P. B. Shelley*)	12
The wind blows out of the gates of the day (*W. B. Yeats*)	99
The woods decay, the woods decay and fall (*A. Tennyson*)	155
There dwelt at the court of a good king (*R. L. Gales*)	71
There was a lady lived in a hall (*W. Morris*)	48
There was an old woman (*W. de la Mare*)	9
There were twa sisters sat in a bour (*Old Ballad*)	55
Tiger, tiger, burning bright (*W. Blake*)	119
We are lilies fair (*Leigh Hunt*)	6
We paused beneath the shadow of the pines (*E. L. Fowler*)	133
What heart could have thought you? (*F. Thompson*)	86
When I was but thirteen or so (*W. J. Turner*)	26
When I went o'er the mountains (*P. MacGill*)	33
When the herds were watching (*W. Canton*)	13
When the spinning-room was here (*W. Allingham*)	43
When think you comes the Wind (*P. B. Marston*)	7
Where am I from? From the green hills of Erin (*M. O'Neill*)	101
Where dips the rocky highland (*W. B. Yeats*)	31
Who passes down the wintry street? (*K. Tynan*)	1
With lifted feet, hands still (*H. C. Beeching*)	23
With sweetest milk and sugar first (*A. Marvell*)	121
Won't you look out of your window, Mrs. Gill? (*W. de la Mare*)	28